The BIG Book of Reading, Rhyming and Resources

The BIG Book of
Reading, Rhyming and Resources

Programs for Children, Ages 4–8

Beth Maddigan
and Stefanie Drennan

Illustrations by Roberta Thompson

LIBRARIES
U N L I M I T E D
A Member of the Greenwood Publishing Group

Westport, Connecticut • London

Library of Congress Cataloging-in-Publication Data

Maddigan, Beth.
    The big book of reading, rhyming, and resources : programs for children, ages 4-8 / Beth
  Maddigan and Stefanie Drennan ; illustrated by Roberta Thompson.
        p. cm.
    Includes bibliographical references and index.
      ISBN 1-59158-220-2 (pbk. : alk. paper)
      1. Children's libraries—Activity programs. 2. Children—Books and reading. 3.
    Libraries and families. 4. Reading promotion. 5. Children's literature—Bibliography.
    I. Drennan, Stefanie. II. Title.
    Z718.1.M257 2005
    027.62'5—dc22   2005016074

British Library Cataloguing in Publication Data is available.

Library of Congress Catalog Card Number: 2005016074
ISBN: 1–59158–220–2

First published in 2005

Libraries Unlimited, 88 Post Road West, Westport, CT 06881
A Member of the Greenwood Publishing Group, Inc.
www.lu.com

Printed in the United States of America

∞

7975

The paper used in this book complies with the Permanent
Paper Standard issued by the National Information
Standards Organization (Z39.48-1984).

10 9 8 7 6 5 4 3 2 1

Contents

Chapter 3: Programs for Fours and Fives (*Cont.*)

Acknowledgments

The success of this book's predecessor, *The Big Book of Stories, Songs, and Sing-Alongs: Programs for Babies, Toddlers, and Families,* is the foundation from which we present this second volume. We would like to thank all those who attended our workshops and conferences. We are grateful for your compliments, criticism, and support. We would like to send our gratitude to everyone who consulted on, reviewed, and used the first volume. We have learned from your feedback and encouragement. We hope you enjoy this second volume and that it provides us with new users that will compliment, criticize, and utilize!

Introduction

Welcome to an adventure in children's programming! Introducing young children to the world of reading, books, and literature is an important job. Teachers, librarians, bookstore employees, caregivers, and parents have been doing it for decades. The way we help children discover the world of reading has evolved over the last century, but the importance of the task has not diminished. In our fast-paced, electronic society the impact of literacy cannot be ignored. Children accept technology as the fabric of their society. Our job as literacy providers is to create a dynamic path to the world of children's literature. We must shed our adult skins and discover the world from a child's perspective. That vision of the world needs to be infiltrated with wisdom in words from great authors and vision in pictures from talented illustrators.

The adventure began for us with predecessor to this book, *The BIG Book of Stories, Songs, and Sing-Alongs: Programs for Babies, Toddlers, and Families,* published by Libraries Unlimited in 2003. This book will take up where the last volume left off, with the next chronological age grouping of children—four and five year olds—and then will continue on to explore programs for six, seven, and eight year olds. We will continue with the popular elements of that format to present you with a guide that prepares you for programming with preschoolers and young school-age children and provides you with ready-to-use sample programs.

Ingredients

The samples in this book provide you with several ingredients for successful programs: Books to Share, Rhymes and Songs, Awesome Activities, Crafty Creations, and Great Games. Some facilities will use all of these ingredients, some will pick and choose activities that suit their mandate, and some will focus on books and use them as read-alouds. We chose a diverse line-up of programming ingredients because we believe the best method to encourage children to read and enjoy children's literature is to build a path that every child can travel. Children learn in a variety of ways determined by their personal physiology: genetics, personality, intelligence, individual experiences, and the world around them. By providing them with a multisensory experience that includes many facets: tactile, visual, auditory, and kinesthetic, we are proving a recipe that appeals to many children from diverse backgrounds and levels of literacy. You may find the recipe needs some adjustment to match the goals and objectives of your institution. As you would with any good cookbook, we expect you to work with the recipe and make it your own. This is the recipe that has been successful for us, successful in a diverse community with a variety of literacy levels and learning styles.

Choices

Every great chef believes he or she has the best formula, combinations, and creations. We have made choices in this book that we believe provide the best combination for a diverse palate. However, we may have a slightly different perspective than that of traditional library programming. This is based on the successful development of programs in our community over the past five years. We took risks, experimented, and chronicled a path of diverse experiences that ended in a set of library programs that are popular and accessible. We began with a traditional library perspective and were given the job of appealing to a wider audience. We were charged with making our library programs more accurately reflect the dynamic institution the public library is today: a place of community meeting, popular materials lending, visual stimuli, forward thinking, and traditional grounding. Our choices are based on several precepts:

- Programs should appeal to participants from different backgrounds with different literacy levels.

- Programs should be multidimensional and appeal to many personalities and learning-styles.

- Children will respond in different ways to different stimuli.

- Popular materials are useful for comfort and familiarity.

- Traditional, exceptional, and award-winning materials are useful to broaden horizons.

- Nonreaders are parents who may want to expose their children to literature-based programming.

- Highly educated readers are parents who may want to expose their children to literature-based programming.

The world is filled with bells and whistles; today's children are exposed to a plethora of stimuli. The programs in this guide keep up with society's pace in a positive way. They are fast-paced and fun-filled. However, they are also designed to provide an escape, a shift in perspective, a new way of looking at the world for children who are busy with school, computers, play dates, and extracurricular activities. These programs provide an introduction to the world of children's literature that bridges modern children's everyday lives.

Style

If you accept the challenge this book presents—to meet children in today's world and provide them with wonderful programs designed to keep pace and enlighten—you will be pleasantly surprised at the results. The authors of this book come from a variety of backgrounds and merged on a playing field that combines the traditional, developmental, dynamic, and popular. Your personal style will lend spice to the mix and help make the programs your own. The way you interact with the children, present the elements, and develop the ingredients will make your programs successful. The excitement this book provides is the excitement you feel when inspired with new ideas and infused with enthusiasm. The premise we base this book upon is that of a fresh perspective on children's literature-based programming. But it is also a successfully demonstrated perspective, one that is proven to appeal to a diverse community and that anchors the idea that the promotion of reading is what programming is all about.

Chapter 1

Program Foundations

As you prepare to introduce young people to the world of books and reading, set aside a little time to think, plan, and develop. To achieve that sense of fun without effort, advance preparation and careful planning are key. Before you begin choosing your books and activities, spend some time thinking about why you are developing these programs, what you are trying to achieve, and who will be attending. By spending a little extra time on the building blocks of your program you will be on your way to successful, polished programs.

1. Keys to Successful Literature-Based Programs

To guarantee success your programs must have a mandate, they should be presented in a style that is easy for children of the appropriate age or grade to relate to, and they need to be constantly evaluated and improved.

1.1 Goals and Objectives

It is fundamental to develop institutional goals for children's programs. And yet, it is so easy to lose sight of our goals as we get caught up in creating amazing programs for children, because the program itself becomes the focus. As dedicated programmers, however, it is our job to ensure we understand *why* we do what we do and keep this in the forefront of our minds as we plan and develop programs. We all know storytime is fun for children and that reading is a good thing, but you need to be more specific and have goals that tie your children's programming line-up back to your facility and your facility's mission statement.

This programming guide is based on the programming model developed at the Cambridge Libraries in Ontario, Canada. The population of this growing city was approximately 100,000 in 2003. In that year, the Cambridge Libraries presented forty-two children's programs per week from its four locations, and approximately 30,000 participants enjoyed those programs over the course of the year. In this system, the library has three children's programming goals. They are described here to give you a sense of direction and purpose for the programs outlined in upcoming chapters. Your facility may have different goals and objectives that will necessitate minor changes and revisions to the programs as outlined.

The first goal of programs presented at the Cambridge Libraries is to create a welcoming environment and positive library experience for participants. Library programmers work hard to make library storytimes familiar and comforting to reduce the intimidation some patrons face upon coming into the library. In Cambridge, low literacy levels and lack of comfort in the library setting are two community factors that drive our programming style. Some people in *your* community are also likely to be intimidated by the public library or school. To combat this staff at the Cambridge Libraries use, circulate, and promote books that some library traditionalists frown upon. We display popular materials right next to the award winners in an effort to get both into the hands, and eventually the homes, of our users. We also use crafts and storytime souvenirs as a marketing tool. These inexpensive giveaways, or process-orientated "make and takes," further the program experience and provide something tangible that serves as a reminder that the library is fun, even if it only hangs on the fridge for a few hours. Although we don't encourage you to think of literature-based programs as "craft time," if crafters leave with an armload of books, you are achieving several of your program's goals.

The second program goal is to provide an introduction to the world of children's literature. This is the goal most literacy specialists will be familiar with: By exposing children to great stories we unlock imaginations and create lifelong readers. This is a well-established goal that most public libraries, elementary schools, and preschools achieve through literature-based programming. However, it is important to keep this goal highlighted to avoid a shift from literature-based programming to entertainment. As we strive to be innovative and come up with great new ideas, we must remember what is important. In Cambridge, we encourage programmers to spend 50 percent of their planning time reading and choosing great books.

Finally, programs should help children and families develop a routine use of the library. This programming goal may be the most important from the public library's perspective, but it is also the most difficult to achieve. In schools and preschools, the focus is a little different, but an emphasis on reading at home is extremely important, regardless of your institution's mandate. In order for literacy to be important for families, the entire family must take an active role in reading outside of school and the library. When this goal is realized through programming, children become independent, confident readers and library users. And families return to the library regularly even after the program is over. However, this goal is challenging to achieve.

Programmers from Canada and the United States who attend workshops based on the first book in this series, *The Big Book of Stories, Songs, and Sing-Alongs*, have expressed concern about patrons who frequent library programs but rarely take out books. In several workshops we have heard programmers complain about patrons who enjoy programs but leave without checking out books to enjoy at home. Through the underlining of this goal, Cambridge Libraries staff were inspired to find creative ways to turn storytime visitors into library users. They developed a number of programming techniques that bring the library home: tours highlighting parenting resources for baby programs, games in after school programs that make use of a number of library collections (including electronic resources), demonstrations in family storytime of electronic products that can be accessed at home. In addition to these "demo-style" ways of helping people learn how to use the library, these programmers developed a set of "at home" reading incentives that have become very successful and popular. Ideas for reading incentives are detailed in the chapters that follow. For the sake of perspective, the types of incentives are outlined here:

BRIGHT IDEA

If you decide to have a prize drawing as an incentive in one of your programs, contact businesses, such as publishers, and ask for a donation to use as a prize. Publishers create promotional materials such as posters, bookmarks, pens, and toys to accompany new books on the market. You won't have any trouble getting publisher freebies if you choose a supplier that you regularly buy books from!

- **Homework**—Give participants specific books and tasks to complete at home. Create bookmarks with fun "at home" projects and place them in books displayed for borrowing. Concentrate on age-appropriate developmental skills that parents are trying to achieve. Display books that can be used at home to practice those skills. Then, discuss success stories in subsequent programs.

- **Challenges**—Give participants a reading task each week; for example, read a poem, learn a joke, or play a word game. The possibilities are endless and can be tied directly back to the theme of your program. Participants who successfully complete the task will get a ticket upon their return to the following program. The ticket will allow them to have their names entered to win a prize. It is amazing what people will do for a contest! Prizes can be tiny, inexpensive things; people simply love hearing their names called when the winning ticket is pulled out.

- **Visual Displays**—Use a repetitive element to create wall art. Hand out simple die cuts or patterned shapes for each book borrowed from the library and read at home. Write the child's name and title of the book on the shape and display it on the wall. Children take pride in watching these interactive displays grow each week.

- **Representational Activities**—Create routine activities that relate to "at home" reading. Every week in a program, spend some time talking about the books children have been reading at home. Then as a group spend a little time building or creating something that represents the reading. Adding jelly beans to a jar or cotton balls to a bunny are examples that have been used successfully in preschool programs.

These are a few of the incentives and encouragements you could use in a program. And once you begin to get into this mindset, you will see how easy it is to create incentives that match your program or theme.

1.2 Child Development

Another key to creating successful literature-based programs is knowledge and understanding of child development. In terms of library programs this refers to matching key skill sets for discrete age groups to the program's ingredients. Programmers need knowledge of child development to develop program routines and plan activities. If your programs are divided into age groupings, take the median age of all the children in your group, look up the developmental skill set for that age, and use those physical and cognitive milestones in your program planning. Keep in mind that children will not have perfected all the skills yet, but generally speaking they will be on their way. The milestones and skills sets for children from four to eight years of age are discussed in detail in the chapters that follow.

1.3 Output Measures and Evaluation

The final key to successful children's programs is evaluation and feedback. Honest feedback from program participants will help you improve your programs and keep them fresh and relevant. You need a way to measure the program's success from the perspective of the participants and parents of participants. It is impossible to do that while you are reading, rhyming, and leading activities. You need a method to solicit feedback. You can do it in a number of ways, but keep in mind that you need to ascertain whether your programs are achieving their specific objectives. It isn't enough to have happy participants, unless your only goal is to create a positive library experience. An evaluation form handed out to the parent of each participant is a great way to get quantifiable responses. The questions should be carefully worded to match the program's objectives and measure success from the library's perspective. The form, which should be simple and straightforward to encourage accurate responses, may be a combination of questions that will elicit qualitative and quantitative results. A sample of the Cambridge Libraries' evaluation form is included in Chapter 6 (see figure 6.5). Evaluation forms, however, are not a perfect solution. In programs for four to eight year olds parents and caregivers are rarely inside, which makes it difficult to evaluate the program's success objectively. Also, people are often more critical when they feel they are anonymous, and some people may have unreasonable expectations and/or strange complaints. Sometimes negative comments can be detrimental to a programmer's confidence. I would not advise using an evaluation form until you have your goals and objectives well established, making sure all programmers are familiar with them and confident that their programs match your institutional objectives. This will give everyone a better sense of *constructive* criticism. In the meantime, if you aren't there yet, there are other great ways to elicit feedback. If you run registered programs, consider calling drop-outs. Get in touch with the people who come once or twice and never come back. Find out why they stopped attending. Another way to elicit participant response is to ask program attendees for informal feedback: for example, what were participant's favourite and least favourite elements? This will work in programs with six to eight year olds, but keep in mind that the children's reasons for coming to a program will be different from your objectives for running the program. Whatever method you choose, make sure you are trying to measure the relative success of your institution's programs. You will be able to use the measured, qualitative responses to secure, or update, your programming line-up.

2. Covering the Basics

Once you have chosen the appropriate type of program you will run, you still have some fundamentals to consider. When will it run? Where will it be held? What do you need to get started? Once you have the basics covered you will be confident and ready to announce your new program to your community.

2.1 Timing of Programs

Programs for four to eight year olds are limited in the times they can be offered. For four and five year olds you will need to find out when kindergarten classes and preschool playgroups are held in your community. Try to find a time slot for your group that complements other programs in your area. This will allow the maximum number of children in your community to attend your program. For six to eight year olds, programs should be held after school. Generally, unless your program is held at school, allow children enough time after getting out to return home, get a snack, and come to your facility. This likely means your program is held at 4:00 or 4:30 in the afternoon. You may choose to have your program right after suppertime. This allows children time to rest, but you will be competing with homework and other family evening rituals. In addition, children may be tired after a long day at school, and after supper they may not be at their best to hone literacy skills. Weekends offer a prime time for school-age children to participate in activities outside of school. However, you should ensure that you are not competing with sports groups and other family weekend activities. You may need to experiment and do a little research before you find the ideal time to offer a new program in your community.

2.2 Choosing a Space

Ideally, programs for four to eight year olds are held in a room designated for such activities. This room should have ample space for a reading circle and physical games, in addition to tables and a work area for arts and crafts and individual activities. If the space has easy access to a sink and washroom, that would be ideal. If your facility doesn't have a designated space and you have to share a space with other activities, be sure to mark out your programming area and explain to children the boundaries they should remain within. For safety reasons, constantly check to make sure all the children remain in the space you have designated for your activities.

2.3 Supplies

To successfully run the programs listed in this text, you will need some basic supplies. If you plan to use the books, games, and activities listed, you will need to have materials such as

- a reading chair;

- an easel and chart paper;

- a magnet board, felt board, and/or chalk board;

- a display table for books to read at home;

- carpet squares or comfy cushions for children to sit on;

- puppets and miscellaneous props; and

- a display area or bulletin board to display reading incentives.

If you plan to use the Crafty Creations included in this book or create other crafts of your own design, you will need a standard set of craft, school, and office supplies on hand as you begin each programming session. Following is a list of the supplies necessary to complete all of the Crafty Creations in this book, plus a few extras. These materials can be found at your local school supply store, hardware store, or local discount or dollar store.

- Adhesive tape
- Aluminium foil
- Beads (various sizes)
- Bingo dabbers
- Brass fasteners
- Brown paper lunch bags
- Buttons
- Cardstock (64 lb. paper)
- CDs (gather them from junk mail and start a collection)
- Chalk
- Confetti
- Construction paper (variety of colours)
- Cotton balls
- Cotton swabs
- Craft sticks—tongue depressors
- Crayons
- Drinking straws (bendable and straight)
- Elastics
- Exacto™ knife
- Feathers
- Feathers (variety of colours)
- Felt (variety of colours)
- Fun foam (variety of colours)
- Gift basket cellophane (variety of colours)
- Glitter
- Glitter glue
- Glue sticks
- Hole punch
- Long craft/bamboo sticks
- Masking tape

- Old puzzle pieces
- Paint brushes
- Paint sticks/stirrers (available free from a local hardware store)
- Painting sponges
- Paper plates (large and small)
- Paper towel rolls
- Party blowers
- Pencil crayons
- Permanent markers—black
- Photocopy paper
- Pinking shears
- Plastic cups
- Pom-poms (variety of colours)
- Popsicle sticks
- Poster board (variety of colours)
- Pipe cleaners (variety of colours)
- Sand (for crafting)
- Scissors
- Sealable baggies
- Stapler
- String
- Styrofoam™ balls
- Styrofoam™ cups (variety of sizes)
- Tissue paper
- Washable markers
- Washable tempera paint
- Waxed paper
- White school glue
- Wiggle eyes (variety of sizes)
- Yarn

In addition to the supplies listed, a few specialty items will be needed: flour, rubbing alcohol, baby barley, dried beans, plastic lids (from margarine containers), vegetable oil, salt, cream of tartar, food colouring, and Kool-Aid (unsweetened). These may be purchased at the grocery store or may be donated by parents, participants, and staff. Remember to plan and ask in advance so that you will have all of the supplies you need on the day of your program.

3. Issues and Answers

Programming with children is a rewarding, fun-filled, and unpredictable career. Children will respond to your direction, learn from your example, and seek out your approval and praise. However, groups of children will also bring challenges. Virtually every programmer faces difficulties leading a group of children. Over the course of a career of leading children's programs, most programmers share similar complaints and challenges. *The BIG Book of Stories, Songs, and Sing-Alongs* details a thorough list of programming problems and how to avoid them for children of all ages. In this chapter we discuss problems specific to leading groups of preschoolers and young school-age children.

3.1 Developing Your Programming Style

It is not unusual to be uncomfortable leading a group of children. This is especially true if you are new to programming. To overcome this discomfort, you must take some time to develop your individual programming style. Analyze what you do well and emphasize those skills in your programs. If you are dramatic, use drama games as an ice-breaker for your group. If you have a gentle, friendly style, share individual time with children as they work on projects. Whatever your strengths, take the time to think about them and enhance your programs by highlighting them.

In addition, you cannot ignore your weaknesses. Some weak points may be integral to programming and you may have to develop techniques to work with your weak points. For example, if you are a terrible singer, you may never be completely comfortable leading a group in song. Does that mean you will never sing in front of a group? Of course not. Music is a wonderful tool to get a group focused and involved. If you're an awful singer, use CDs or a karaoke machine and enlist the help of the entire group for a sing-along. Alternatively, you could use a puppet with a funny voice to lead the singing. Children will know the puppet is a terrible singer, but they won't have a clue if you can sing or not!

Some programmers feel nervous reading stories to a group. To overcome a jittery reading voice, read your stories *aloud* before you go into your program. Every programmer chooses books he or she enjoys and has read before, but by reading the book *aloud* before you go into the program you will identify trouble spots or difficult phrases and have a chance to practice and perfect them.

These are just a couple of examples of strengths and weaknesses. Think about your personal attributes. Find out what works for you, adapt it to a variety of age levels, and then keep a stock of tried and true favourites on hand to use any time you begin to feel uncomfortable or out of your element. As you grow more and more confident, try new things, go beyond your comfort zone, and explore new programming techniques. Challenge yourself—you'll never get bored or tired of programming, and your repertoire will grow and stay relevant.

3.2 Encouraging Group Participation

Sometimes participants in your group will be shy or difficult to draw into the mix. This becomes more evident in groups of older children. Once they reach school age, children tend to be more self-conscious. In addition, some children are naturally shy. This problem may crop up in groups of preschoolers as well. To make everyone in your group feel welcome and comfortable, give each child a few moments of special attention. This can be done at the beginning when you greet the children and again while children are working on individual projects.

Sometimes you need to work a little harder to make children feel comfortable interacting with one another. To assist this process, play games that require every child to participate in a nonthreatening way. For example, you might try playing the spotlight game. In a darkened room, shine a flashlight around the room while chanting:

Spotlight, spotlight is the name of the game
When the spot lands on you, tell us your name.

Have the flashlight's spot land on every child in a random order and have each one call out his or her name. Begin by shining the light on children you sense will not feel intimidated, and once the group gets the hang of it, draw out some of the shyer children.

You could also try activities that require a leader and change the leader every time you play. The first time choose a leader who is comfortable in front of the group. After the children have played a couple of times and are enjoying the game, choose a leader who is less outgoing and let him or her have a turn. An example of this type of game is Frog Fairy. As the leader, you are the special frog fairy. When you wave your magic wand, all the frog children will be under your spell and will have to do as you say. You'll need one frog to be the leader and demonstrate what all the others should do. The leader gets to wear a special crown or hat, and it is his or her job to show the group how to do the actions. Explain that the first action will be hopping. Have the leader show the group how frogs hop. Then wave your magic wand and begin to chant:

> Hop, hop little froggies, hop, hop.
> Hop, hop little froggies, hop, hop.
> Hop, hop little froggies,
> Hop, hop little froggies,
> Hop, hop little froggies, hop, hop!

Ask the leader whether he or she thought the group did a good job. Then give the group another chance by having the froggies sing. How do froggies sing? Well, by saying, "Ribbit," of course. Have the leader demonstrate his or her loudest "Ribbit." Then begin to chant:

> Sing, sing little froggies, sing, sing: *ribbit, ribbit*
> Sing, sing little froggies, sing, sing: *ribbit, ribbit*
> Sing, sing little froggies,
> Sing, sing little froggies,
> Sing, sing little froggies, sing, sing: *ribbit, ribbit*

Froggies can also dance and laugh and do lots of other things, but at the end they usually sleep. Change the leader for every second or third action and play the game several times over the course of a four- to eight-week program so that every child will have a turn as the leader.

3.3 Overcrowding

Occasionally your programs will be very popular, and large numbers of participants will want to attend. To avoid large crowds in programs, run programs that require preregistration. This will allow you to control the group's number, and you'll have a consistent set of children attending each week. If you plan to have adults drop children off and leave them in your care, preregistration is required. In these cases you will also need to limit attendance based on the legal restriction for the number of children one adult can have in his or her care outside of the formal school setting. Most public libraries require parents to remain in the building while their children attend a program. In these cases you must have strict limits based on the program's requirements and the size of the space where the program is held. When you are registering children, keep the size of the group optimal and don't be concerned if you have a waiting list. Waiting lists are inevitable with popular programs. And, if you also offer drop-in programs at a different time, participants have alternatives. For those drop-in programs, prepare for large crowds. Limit numbers based on room size by handing out free tickets and admitting advance ticket holders first.

3.4 Developmental Discrepancies

If you have done children's programs for a year or more, you have probably met the parents who genuinely believe their four year old should be in the six-year-old program. Unfortunately, love can cloud judgement, so parents are not always in the best position to judge their child's skill level. Therefore, you will need to choose a more objective way to limit the attendance in your program so children are all on roughly the same level. You may choose to run your programs based on child development principles, for example, readers in one group, pre-readers in another. More commonly, we use age restrictions to define our programs. If you use the age-defining method, offer programs in a series and present each series three or four times a year in six-, eight-, or ten-week groupings. Potential participants may not get into the program they want because their birth dates fall outside the range, but in the next session a few months later, they will be able to attend.

3.5 Latecomers

One of the most problematic programming situations is caused by the participant who arrives ten minutes after a program begins and boisterously pushes his or her child into the program room. This is disruptive for the program and embarrassing for the child. To avoid this problem, express your expectations for arrival before the program and speak to adult latecomers directly every time a problem arises. Occasionally, people do have a valid reason for being late—car trouble, a delayed train, an upset baby sibling. Speak to the adult who brought the child to the program late immediately afterward on the very occasion that they are late and explain how difficult it can be to keep the attention of a large group of children. Allow the adult to explain the situation and, if it is a one-time happening, which it will often be if you deal with the problem head on, simply let it go. People respond to directness, especially if it is presented in a nonthreatening manner. Try a friendly tone and say something like, "Did you have trouble getting here today?" and wait for the explanation. After it comes, explain, "It's really hard in the middle of a story to make a new child feel welcome. And when someone comes in after a program begins it can be disruptive for the group." Leave it at that and monitor the situation. If it happens again, unless the excuse is truly exceptional, take a harder line on the second offence. Finally, don't be afraid to end a session for chronic latecomers. Look at your program schedule and offer alternatives, if possible, for program times at another location or at a different time that might be more accessible for them.

3.6 Discipline

Another problem every programmer encounters from time to time is a child who misbehaves. Because parents and caregivers are not inside the program room, children occasionally become disruptive and act out. Your method for handling discipline will depend on your facility's level of responsibility for the care of the child. In schools and community care facilities, the parents will not be present in the building. In these situations discipline is the responsibility of the adult leading the group. In public libraries, however, discipline is still the responsibility of the parents, even if they are not in direct sight of their children. If possible, use a volunteer or an assistant in a public library program to help with discipline. While you lead the group, the assistant takes the disruptive child out to the waiting parent or caregiver and explains the problem. Sometimes it is not possible because of staffing and budget considerations to have a second staff member in every program. In these cases you still need to come up with a method to give children with serious behaviour issues back to their accompanying adults to handle. Discipline should never be the focus of a program, and adults should be instructed to remain nearby to deal with problems. Some minor discipline issues can be tackled by separating children who misbehave or by having a child who is not focused be a "helper" with specific duties. However, the best way to deal with behaviour issues is to discuss them directly with the adult who accompanies the child to the program and come up with a clear, simple plan of action. Have the adult discuss appropriate behaviour with the child before the next program. Talking about it at home can clear up some misconceptions the child might have. If the behaviour issue was serious, such as a child hitting another child, include in the plan a method to reintegrate the child slowly to independent participation in the group. For example, in a preschool storytime, you might have the supervising adult accompany and sit with the child for a week or two. Then the adult may gradually be able to sit near the back and, finally, leave the program area altogether. If the behaviour resurfaces when the child is once again unsupervised, you'll have to speak to the supervising adult and explain that the child is not ready for the program at this time and that you would be happy to welcome the child back in the next session.

4. The Adventure Begins

Take a deep breath and get ready to have fun! Four to eight year olds are individuals who understand what they like and don't like. They can occasionally be tough critics. However, if you are enjoying yourself and having fun, they will respond to the positive energy and will be much more likely to have fun, too. Choose activities, games, books, and materials that you enjoy and feel comfortable with. Share your love of books and literature with the children by inspiring and enlightening them. Never be afraid to make mistakes. Children will not judge you for saying the wrong word or giving garbled instructions. The ability to laugh at yourself is the first step to having an entire group of children laugh right along with you!

Chapter 2

Fours and Fives: Program Preparations

Preschool storytime is standard fare in public libraries. This type of program is also commonly found in community centres, preschools, and even bookstores. Virtually all community libraries offer a program for children aged three to five years. This book begins with a chapter on preschool storytime, but it is focused on *four and five year olds*. Where are the three year olds? Hopefully you will find them in a preschool storytime program designed specifically for their age group. Three year olds do best in a transitional program designed specifically to assist them with independent group settings. To find out how to design a program just for three year olds, refer to *The BIG Book of Stories, Songs, and Sing-Alongs: Programs for Babies, Toddlers, and Families* (Maddigan et al., 2003).

Four and five year olds are generally able to interact in a group setting away from the direct line of sight of a parent or familiar caregiver. They have likely attended preschool, birthday parties, and day camps. At some point between their fourth and seventh birthdays, most children will enter school and begin their formal education in a classroom with twenty or more classmates and one teacher. Therefore, some administrators may ask if the library still needs to offer storytime for four and five year olds, because formalized education is responsible for the socialization process and development of emergent literacy skills. The answer is a resounding yes. Library programming is about more than socialization and a preamble to school. It is important to continue library programming even after formal education has begun for children because

- the library offers a relaxed and pressure-free environment to begin the enjoyment of literature—no tests, skills-assessment, or grades;

- the public library can provide extra support and encouragement for education;

- library storytimes allow children a chance to read and learn for fun and pure enjoyment, and the importance of play for children's mental development has been widely documented (Mustard, 1999);

- library storytimes are shorter and have fewer attendees than the classroom setting;

- many children at this stage of development respond positively to a limited time span and restricted number of peers; and

- many children are relaxed and comfortable at the library because they have been visiting the library since babyhood. Comfort in a setting will make the environment more conducive to a positive experience.

Storytime in a public library, community center, or school should be a place for children to come and enjoy their introduction to the literary world, regardless of the individual skills they bring with them. They should be allowed to experience the joys of reading at their own pace with little or no expectation for performance or achievement.

Four and five year olds are at the prime age to begin to enjoy the world of literature. Because these children are ready for an expanded worldview, the focus of storytime shifts slightly. Programs for children three years and under generally focus on having the children participate as a part of a group. Storytime for four and five year olds, however, focuses on children participating in a group setting as individuals. The difference is subtle but very important. At this age children are ready to express ideas and opinions as well as share personal experiences. They should be encouraged to make individual choices within the framework of the group. There is still plenty of room for group activities that involve a singular experience, but when the opportunity presents itself, children should be encouraged to express their own opinion or choose their roles in an activity or game.

1. What Can Four and Five Year Olds Do?: Child Development for Fours and Fives

The period between forty-eight and seventy-two months of age is quite broad and includes many developmental milestones. So you may wonder why we have decided to group both years together. The rationale is still based on cognitive development. The tools children need to enjoy a traditionally structured preschool storytime include approximately a ten-minute attention span, the ability to participate in organized play, and an understanding of rules. These milestones are often achieved by children as they reach the forty-six- to fifty-month span. However, these benchmarks can, and in fact should, be reinforced and nurtured for the next several years. Children at the older end of this age group will often be more accomplished at listening and responding to direction. Younger children will benefit and learn by modeling this behaviour.

We have discussed the fact that four and five year olds achieve many important milestones that will be nurtured, tested, and improved over the coming years. But what are they, specifically? What can four- and five-year-old children do?

At forty-eight months many children have just begun to

- recognize letters of the alphabet;

- count in sequence out loud,

- understand spatial concepts such as over, under, tallest, and smallest;

- speak in complex sentences;

- question the world around them;

- develop a ten-minute attention span;

- dress themselves with minimal assistance;

- enjoy playing with other children for extended periods; and

- develop their imaginations and sense of humour.

Similarly, after their fourth birthdays children continue to expand on these milestones and reach others. By sixty months many children have begun to

- use and identify letters of the alphabet and numbers;

- master spatial concepts as well as relationships among people;

- use a large vocabulary and speak in full sentences;

- develop a longer attention span, as long as fifteen minutes for some tasks;

- become project minded and be able to plan and create things from start to finish;

- enjoy making their own decisions, taking turns, and following directions;

- notice and be sensitive to the feelings of others; and

- develop a sense of humour and a sense of story development.

Four- and five-year-old children have developed a key new ability for storytime—imagination. They can now truly appreciate a world beyond their own. They understand that imaginary characters and settings are not real, but they enjoy listening and becoming captivated by them. Helping children to embrace and develop their imaginative side is a key ingredient in assisting children with their creative development. By exposing them to the literary world you are giving them the keys to travel everywhere! By empowering children to explore beyond the confines of their own existence, we help them to begin to develop their potential. They understand that they can become, learn about, and discover anything their minds can contemplate. Their imaginations become key to creative thought and personal exploration.

2. Four and Five Year Old Programming Guidelines

2.1 Starting a Program for Four and Five Year Olds

Historically, the first book-based programs offered by many libraries and community centers was preschool storytime (Nespeca, 1994). Traditionally, this program for children from three to five years old is a preamble to formal schooling, as we discussed in the last section. However, the programming model we have set up in this manual requires it to be much, much more. By separating the three year olds into their own program, you will allow yourself much greater potential for program development for four and five year olds. Ideally, your program will require preregistration. If you know the children coming to the program you will be better able to structure activities and games. The children will enjoy the program more because they will have a chance to become comfortable and familiar with their fellow participants. If they know what to expect from the program's routine and from the other attendees, children will be more likely to participate, relax, and enjoy themselves. Although a preregistered program is the ideal, this age group is also well-suited to drop-in programs. Four and five year olds are typically comfortable with group situations, as many of them have attended other library programs or preschool. Most of these children can adapt quite easily to unfamiliar surroundings and people. However, each session should include a brief social or "get to know you" period at the beginning.

If your center does not provide a program for four and five year olds, introducing one is simple. Children at this age need the stimulation and creativity boost that the storytime atmosphere provides. The only major obstacle to adopting this program is competition from other venues such as junior kindergarten or preschool programming at other centers. Vying with other centers that specialize in programming for young children is a reality, but a good marketing program should draw people into your center (see Chapter 6 for details). Once children experience a quality literature-based program, the benefits will be obvious and their caregivers will enthusiastically return for future programs.

2.2 Getting Ready

There are a few key concepts to keep in mind when you are preparing for a program with four and five year olds. Children will be sitting for extended periods of time, so they should have a comfortable carpet, mats, cushions, or child-sized chairs to sit on. In order to read longer stories, you will have to include gross motor activities before and after the lengthy tales, so your area should have lots of open space. You will also want to focus on creative endeavours such as free-form music and art activities. If possible, invest in a set of musical instruments, paint, art supplies, and smocks. Use these tools to help children exercise their newly acquired creative side with open-ended, unstructured activities.

Bright Idea

If your facility does not have a budget for program supplies such as musical instruments or art smocks, you can make your own: chopsticks can double as rhythm sticks, and old adult-sized T-shirts make great cover-ups during messy activities.

Add value and excitement to this program by introducing tools such as

- a magnet board, felt board, and/or chalk board for visual storytelling;
- a cassette or CD player to add music for dancing or background music while children are enjoying arts and crafts or other individual activities;
- an easel or prop board to display oversized books while you read them aloud to the group;
- a storytelling apron or smock to hide props or items for show and tell activities;
- puppets, stuffed toys, and props for dramatic play; and
- costumes, hats, crowns, and scarves for dress-up and pretend play.

These are just a few of the extra items and enhancements you may choose to include in your storytime. Although none of these is a necessary element, each will allow you to add something extra to your program.

2.2a Emergent Literacy

Emergent literacy is a phrase commonly used in relation to early childhood language and prereading skill development (Walter, 2001). Although the terminology is relatively new, the concept has been around in library programs for decades. Also known as "reading readiness," its fundamental philosophy is that children, before they are able to read words on a page, can benefit from exposure to literature, reading, books, and stories. This exposure will help prepare them for the transition to independent reading when they are intellectually ready. By exposing preschoolers with developing imaginations and attention spans to books, words, stories, and illustrations, you are helping them to understand reading even before they can do it themselves. Five year olds, for example, begin to understand that reading occurs from left to right. Although they are not yet able to understand the words, they are familiar and comfortable with the concept of reading. This enables them to be more confident when it comes time to try reading on their own.

While you are preparing your program, the concept of emergent literacy should be lurking somewhere in the back of your mind. You won't be teaching children how to read, but you will be introducing them to the idea that reading is exciting and fun. When children begin to make the sometimes difficult transition to reading on their own, these positive literary experiences will remind them that it is worth all the effort.

2.2b Books to Share

Four year olds have begun to develop their imaginations and can appreciate stories with imaginary concepts. Five-year-old children will enjoy the same stories and will often appreciate some dimensions missed by the younger children. For example, the story *Something from Nothing* by Phoebe Gilman is a wonderful tale of a boy and his grandfather. There is a subplot to the text of this story that is developed in the pictures. Gilman has illustrated a family of mice who live on the edges of the page. These mice have an adventure of their own that is told in the pictures. Five year olds will appreciate this whimsical subplot as well as the main storyline. Four year olds are less likely to notice the story of the mice unless it is pointed out to them. This book shows some of the characteristics you should look for in read-aloud stories for four and five year olds: extra dimensions, more complex themes, and subtext. Another book with a story in the pictures and a more complex plot is *Officer Buckle and Gloria*. Four and five year olds will be amused by the antics of Gloria the police dog, who performs tricks outside of the text, which focuses on Officer Buckle's safety tips.

To stimulate four- and five-year-old children, look for books and stories that achieve excellence in a number of different areas:

- use of language,

- sound of text when read aloud,

- characterization,

- plot development (including a satisfactory conclusion), and

- placement and style of illustrations.

At this age children appreciate many themes in a story and are no longer constrained by the things they can relate to in the world around them. There are many story "types" you can look for to entertain children at this age, including

- humorous stories;

- silly or fantastic stories;

- stories with a "pleasant surprise" ending;

- cumulative stories (stories with repetitive refrains that build upon one another, like the classic *The House That Jack Built*);

- family stories, including those about families very different from their own;

- child-centered stories, especially those that feature the child as the hero of the story; and

- animal stories (these are popular with virtually any age).

2.2c Books to Display

Four- and five-year-old children enjoy a wide range of books, and a display of samples to take home should include

- any book you would consider suitable to read aloud;

- longer stories such as fairytales and folktales (children are able to appreciate longer books when they are read one on one);

- concept books, especially those focusing on the alphabet, numbers, shapes, and colors;

- simple nonfiction books on topics of interest such as animals, transportation, and children from other countries;

- poetry and rhyme books, especially those with simple nonsense verse; and

- joke books with simple text.

Encourage children to take these books home and share them with the adults who love them; this will allow families to continue the storytime experience at home.

2.2d Reading Incentives

Sometimes displays of books and encouragement are not enough to convince busy families of the importance of reading at home. By including a reading incentive in your program, you will tie sharing books at home back to the program. You will also encourage a routine use of the library that children will convince their parents to continue long after the program is over. An effective incentive for children at this age is large visuals that they can help build on. For example, if your program takes place in the winter, build a large snowman on the wall. For each book read at home the children add a cotton ball to the snowman. Over the weeks of the program children will watch as the snowman fills in, and at the end of the season the snowman will be a fuzzy wall display that reminds children of their accomplishments during storytime. Use any large visual that fits with your theme, such as a one-dimensional paper train that winds its way around the library. Children may take home train cars, and the adults at home can help by writing the child's name and the title of each book read aloud. Each week the completed cars are added to the train, and children will delight in watching it chug its way around the room. Other examples are apples on a tree, flowers in a meadow, scoops on an ice cream cone, fish in the sea, and stars in the sky. Finding a visual to match your program's themes or season will be easy, but keep in mind that the tangible elements that children will attach to the visual should be simple to mass produce, because you may have to hand out hundreds of them before the program is over!

2.2e Learning Children's Names

Preregistration is important for this age group because it will allow you to design identifiers, such as name tags, and begin to familiarize yourself with children's names. Using a child's name makes him or her feel special and deserving of the attention. It will also serve as a valuable disciplinary tool for the programmer. You will be able to quietly call a disruptive child's name. This individual attention helps overcome unacceptable behaviour.

As children mature as individuals, their names become more and more important. When you are familiarizing yourself with the names of the children, make sure you know how to pronounce them. If you aren't sure about a pronunciation, speak to the child's parent a few minutes before the start of the program, or ask the child to say it first. Saying a child's name correctly helps the child to trust you and feel special. If you do mispronounce a child's name, you will quickly realize it by the child's reaction (or lack of response). Simply apologize for the mistake and ask the child to correct you. Repeat the child's name back to him or her and wait for an affirmative reaction. Repeat the name a few times during the week to avoid getting it wrong the next time.

EXPERT ADVICE

If your facility has a digital or instant camera, use it to take a picture of each of the children in your program while they are wearing their name tags or identifiers. Use these pictures to help you learn children's names. Then, as a special treat for the last week of the program, frame the pictures with bristol board and have the children decorate the frames.

3. Programs for Four and Five Year Olds: Format and Routine

Most four and five year olds are ready to experience social situations with their peers. Few parents and caregivers will feel the need to accompany their children into the program. You should encourage those who do come into the program to leave their children when they are comfortable. Some of the children will be experienced storytimers; others will have experienced similar situations in kindergarten or preschool; for a few of the children it may be their first independent peer group experience. They will take their cues from the more experienced program participants, and the routine for the group will quickly fall into place.

At this age, it is often individual personality traits that set children apart from the group, not a lack of socialization or peer interaction skills. It is a delightful experience to get to know the children and watch their individual personalities emerge as you make them feel special.

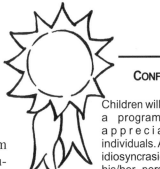

CONFIDENCE BOOSTER

Children will appreciate you as a program leader, if you appreciate them as individuals. Accept each child's idiosyncrasies as a part of his/her personal growth and development. Don't try to force them to conform to the group for every activity. By allowing creative personal expression you will help children develop a strong sense of themselves.

As the group leader, your programming role should have a focus. Although four and five year olds appreciate an accomplished entertainer, they benefit from the storytime experience in specific and measurable ways if a facilitator leads them. To move into this new role, choose activities that focus on the children's involvement instead of your own. Part educator, part entertainer, part ringleader: the facilitator of storytime for a group of four and five year olds is dynamic and flexible.

3.1 Format

The format of your program will depend on your individual style, but a number of fun literacy-related exercises and activities can be included in the time allotted for your group each week. Some of the ingredients will be familiar to you and to most of the children: stories, rhymes, songs, fingerplays, and circle games. The specifics chosen, however, can be longer, more intricate, and contain more complex elements than those you would choose if three year olds were involved in the program. A typical storytime formatted for four and five year olds could run as follows:

1. Opening routine
2. Longest story
3. Songs
4. Circle game
5. Story
6. Fingerplays
7. Action rhymes
8. Other activities/crafts
9. Closing routine

This format can be varied as needed to include room for your personal style. For example, a programmer with a penchant for puppets and drama might design his or her format as follows:

1. Opening routine
2. Longest story
3. Interactive drama game (based on story)
4. Songs
5. Lap puppet theatre
6. Action rhymes
7. Story
8. Other activities/crafts
9. Closing routine

Programmers should feel that they can design a format that includes a showcase for their individual strengths, such as music, drama, puppetry, movement, or dance. Those of us without a particular skill or strength can experiment with a variety of elements and structures, thereby designing a formula or format that works for us.

3.2 Opening Routine

A variety of dynamic and exciting routines can be used to give children their identifiers and begin storytime. Name tags as identifiers and a song to open the program are the most common opening routines. Other openings also work well; for example, pretend play is an excellent concept to enhance children's developing imaginations. Dress-up is a form of pretend play, and if you put each child's name on a crown or special hat, he or she will be able to enjoy pretend play at the beginning of each program. The crown is an excellent example of an identifier that allows children to feel special as individuals (all the crowns are personalized with the children's names), but it also helps them feel part of the group as all the other children in the room are wearing similar identifiers. To match crowns with the appropriate children, line crowns up on a table or counter with the names facing front. Pick up each crown and ask for help from the crowd to find its owner. Say the first part of the child's name, with heavy emphasis on the first syllable or few letters. Children will quickly learn to finish the name as you begin it. They will feel important and special as they supply their names while you are trying to sound out the first few letters.

After each child has a crown, begin storytime with the following rhyme:

Kings and queens and princes, too
Now storytime begins for you.
Straighten your crown,
And sit right down,
And here is what we will do . . .

Launch into a discussion about the theme of storytime after the rhyme is complete. Alternatively, you could design a visual to represent the theme of storytime and as you say the last line of the rhyme, you hold up the visual and have children guess the storytime theme.

3.3 Structure

Although formats and routines can differ, structure is still a very important concept in storytime for four and five year olds. Children will be comforted by the routine and will, therefore, be more open to learning and developing their individual skills. Children at this age are more likely to enjoy surprises, but you should discuss the fact that there will be a surprise to look forward to as an element of the program. For example, you could play an interactive circle game such as *What Is in the Box?* For this game a box is placed in the center of the circle and clues are given to its contents. When the surprise is revealed, it should be the segue into the next element of the program, a puppet or sample craft, for example.

BRIGHT IDEA

Using visuals to represent program themes is a simple way to enhance a program. These visuals can be pictures or props that will help children guess what storytime is about. If your theme is farmyard, you could bring in a stuffed barnyard animal you have at home, or a picture of a barn. The visuals should be fairly simple and obvious, and you can even supply clues to steer children quickly onto the right track. Real objects, such as a pair of mittens used as a prop in a winter storytime, are known as realia. Choose realia familiar to the children to help guide them to the name of each week's theme.

3.4 Print Materials

Although adults do not attend the program, they need to be informed about weekly themes, structure, and important elements. A brochure that includes a message to parents and caregivers, a detailed account of weekly themes, and any special instructions for a given week should be included. For example, you may decide to include a bedtime theme and ask all children to come to the program in their pyjamas. This information should be included on your brochure so parents are less likely to forget on the day of the pyjama party. Print materials should also include details about any food and treats you are planning to give out to children so that adults can tell you about allergies and food sensitivities.

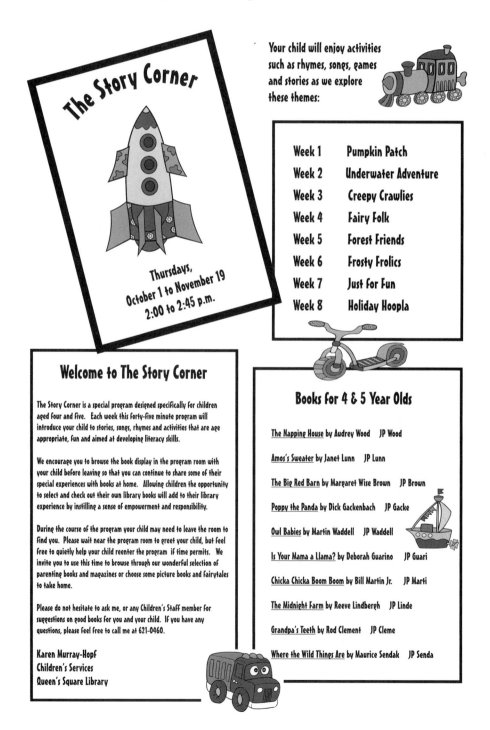

The Story Corner

Thursdays,
October 1 to November 19
2:00 to 2:45 p.m.

Your child will enjoy activities such as rhymes, songs, games and stories as we explore these themes:

Week 1	Pumpkin Patch
Week 2	Underwater Adventure
Week 3	Creepy Crawlies
Week 4	Fairy Folk
Week 5	Forest Friends
Week 6	Frosty Frolics
Week 7	Just For Fun
Week 8	Holiday Hoopla

Welcome to The Story Corner

The Story Corner is a special program designed specifically for children aged Four and Five. Each week this forty-five minute program will introduce your child to stories, songs, rhymes and activities that are age appropriate, fun and aimed at developing literacy skills.

We encourage you to browse the book display in the program room with your child before leaving so that you can continue to share some of their special experiences with books at home. Allowing children the opportunity to select and check out their own library books will add to their library experience by instilling a sense of empowerment and responsibility.

During the course of the program your child may need to leave the room to find you. Please wait near the program room to greet your child, but feel free to quietly help your child reenter the program if time permits. We invite you to use this time to browse through our wonderful selection of parenting books and magazines or choose some picture books and fairytales to take home.

Please do not hesitate to ask me, or any Children's Staff member for suggestions on good books for you and your child. If you have any questions, please feel free to call me at 621-0460.

Karen Murray-Hopf
Children's Services
Queen's Square Library

Books for 4 & 5 Year Olds

The Napping House by Audrey Wood   JP Wood

Amos's Sweater by Janet Lunn   JP Lunn

The Big Red Barn by Margaret Wise Brown   JP Brown

Poppy the Panda by Dick Gackenbach   JP Gacke

Owl Babies by Martin Waddell   JP Waddell

Is Your Mama a Llama? by Deborah Guarino   JP Guari

Chicka Chicka Boom Boom by Bill Martin Jr.   JP Marti

The Midnight Farm by Reeve Lindbergh   JP Linde

Grandpa's Teeth by Rod Clement   JP Cleme

Where the Wild Things Are by Maurice Sendak   JP Senda

3.5 Closing Routine

To end the program you can reverse the opening and have each child place his or her crown on the table or counter. End the program each week with the following rhyme:

Kings and queens and princes too.
Now I must say goodbye to you.
Goodbye, good day, good night and so long,
See you next week for more stories and songs!

4. Four and Five Year Old Programming Techniques

Older children have a longer attention span and the ability to understand complex concepts. Programmers can use these developmental achievements to design dynamic and fun-filled programs.

4.1 Extended Time Period

Four and five year olds are able to enjoy longer stories and more intricate crafts. Therefore, they can remain in the program for a longer period of time. Forty-five minutes or a full hour are appropriate time spans depending upon the activities you choose to include. The formats discussed in the last section will run approximately forty-five minutes. If you include a snack or social activity, the program will last for one hour.

4.2 Including Complex Elements

One of the exciting additions to programs for children at this age is multilayered games and routines. Four and five year olds can follow directions, play games, and enjoy activities more complex than the follow-the-leader style routines that three year olds enjoy. Traditional games, such as *Statues* (children dance and wiggle until the music stops, then they must be still until the music begins again) or *Simon Says* (children follow directions called out by the leader, only if preceded by the phrase, "Simon says . . .") are good examples of possibilities for storytime. These can be adapted to enhance a story or fit a theme.

Other complex elements that are suitable for this age group are

- crafts with multiple steps to completion;

- activities that have the children suggesting, drawing, or designing alternate story endings;

- interactive songs or rhymes with movements, imitation, and repetitive phrases;

- open-ended activities that allow children to use their imaginations to answer a question or complete a problem; and

- puzzles and simple design activities.

These are a few of the many, many complex tasks that four and five year olds enjoy and find challenging at the same time.

4.3 Discussions and Follow-up

Four and five year olds have begun to find their voice and enjoy using it to tell stories and share exciting moments from their lives. After reading a book to the group, it can be beneficial to ask children a series of questions and allow them time to think and share their thoughts and opinions. The follow-up questions can be very simple, especially to get the ball rolling. For example:

- What was the best part of the story?

- What do you think was the funniest thing that happened to <character's name>?

- Did you like what <character's name> did in the story? Why?

You can ask specific questions about elements of the story to foster discussion, but the best questions are open ended with no correct answer. For example, after reading *Curious George* you could ask the children what they think George will do for his next adventure. Or you could ask them what type of animal the man with the yellow hat might have adopted if he had not met George. This type of question fosters creativity as well as stimulating reading comprehension. Follow-up discussions give children a chance to share thoughts and opinions. As the programmer you should be prepared to draw out shy children and to develop a kind way of keeping a boisterous child's speeches to a minimum.

4.4 Dramatic Play

Preschool children have developed imaginations and enjoy using them. One way to help children explore their imaginations is to encourage them in dramatic play. Give children a set of instructions that include acting out their responses to a question. For example, you could ask children to think of their favourite pet and act like that animal. Then ask them to move around the room, finding other animals that are the same as they are. At the end of a crazy few minutes you should have a group of cats, a group of dogs, and the odd hamster and fish rounding out the group. Children enjoy silly antics, especially those that allow them to use their imaginations in ways that are interesting and new.

4.5 Making Each Child Feel Special

Four and five year olds need attention and a chance to have the spotlight on them as individuals. You can achieve this by learning children's names and using them to call each child for his or her turn in an activity or game. You can also involve individual children by having each child provide something to complete an activity. In the autumn, for example, you could have each child add a coloured leaf to a tree you have on display. Or give each child an apple slice to colour and have him or her add it to a pie crust that you paste on the wall.

Another way to make each child feel special is to greet each one individually and to point out something to make them all feel happy about themselves. This could be as simple as commenting on Jimmy's sneakers or Jenny's careful colouring. Individual attention, presented in a casual, friendly manner, helps children gain confidence and feel comfortable in their surroundings.

4.6 Concentrating on Literacy

Programming for children in this age range has limitless possibilities. To provide focus for your program and keep it centered on your facility's objectives, you will likely need to concentrate on book-based activities. This does not mean storytime will consist only of stories. Focus your efforts on language, poetry, rhyme, and song as well as creativity-building activities. By stimulating children in a literary way, you help to set the stage for reading, writing, and comprehension. For libraries, you are building future users who will remember your institution with fondness and respect.

5. Bibliography of Books to Share

Brown, Margaret Wise. 1989. *The Big Red Barn*. New York: HarperCollins.

Clement, Rod. 1997. *Grandad's Teeth*. Sydney, Australia: HarperCollins.

Gackenbach, Dick. 1984. *Poppy the Panda*. New York: Clarion Books.

Gilman, Phoebe. 1992. *Something from Nothing: Adapted from the Jewish Folktale*. Richmond Hill, ON: North Winds Press.

Guarino, Deborah. 1989. *Is Your Mama a Llama?* New York: Scholastic.

Lindbergh, Reeve. 1987. *The Midnight Farm*. New York: Dial Books for Young Readers.

Lunn, Janet. 1988. *Amos's Sweater*. Vancouver, BC: Douglas & McIntyre.

Martin, Bill, Jr. 1989. *Chicka Chicka Boom Boom*. New York: Simon & Schuster.

Mayo, Diana. 2001. *The House That Jack Built*. New York: Barefoot Books.

Rathmann, Peggy. 1995. *Officer Buckle and Gloria*. New York: G. P. Putnam's Sons.

Rey, H. A. 1969. *Curious George*. Boston: Houghton Mifflin.

Sendak, Maurice. 1984. *Where the Wild Things Are*. New York: Harper & Row.

Waddell, Martin. 1992. *Owl Babies*. Cambridge, MA: Candlewick Press.

Wood, Audrey. 1984. *The Napping House*. San Diego: Harcourt Brace Jovanovich.

Chapter 3

Programs for Fours and Fives

The programs in this chapter are designed to foster the growth of young minds and help develop life-long readers. Every aspect of these programs, from the games and activities to the crafts, is merely an extension of our main purpose as educators and facilitators. That purpose is to build and maintain an interest in the joy of reading and listening to stories read aloud. Most four and five year olds are content to sit and have a story read to them, but a few key things to remember when choosing stories to read aloud to this age group follow.

- **Vocabulary**—Are the words easy to understand? If children can't understand a story, how can they be expected to sit and listen to it?

- **Illustrations**—Are the pictures visible from a distance? Are they detailed enough to hold the children's attention, but not so busy that they won't have time to see the whole picture before the page is turned (causing them to lose interest)?

- **Repetitive Stories and Child Involvement**—Is there a way to involve the children in the story? Is there a phrase that the children can anticipate and repeat with you? Are there questions that you can ask before turning the page to see what the children think will happen next (e.g., *Mortimer* by Robert Munsch)?

- **Interest**—Did you choose the book because you like to read it or because you thought your group would enjoy it? Once you begin your programs and try out a few different styles of books (rhyming, repetitive, etc.), you'll gain a better understanding of what your group will enjoy listening to.

One final thing to remember when reading to this or any age group is style and delivery. The more involved you get in telling the story, the more the children in your group will want to listen to it (perhaps even over and over again). One handy tip is to practice reading the book before you present it in your program and try using different voices and voice levels for the different characters in the story. Speaking loudly, or hushed, stamping feet, or clapping where appropriate will keep your group's eyes and attention focused on the pages before them.

Note: Some of the programs that follow are based on holidays or days that are celebrated, such as Hallowe'en. It is important to remember that not everyone in your programs will be either celebrating or partaking in any or all of the festivities planned on these days. One way to inform the parents and caregivers of this is to send home a note approximately two weeks in advance, advising them of the program theme and what will be happening on that day, so that you will know whether you will have any absences.

Let's Get Started!

We begin our programming for four and five year olds with a session about fall. The programs in this chapter each contain eight songs, rhymes, or fingerplays; two crafts; and one game and/or activity per theme, as well as a list of what we consider to be a few good books to share. Programs with this age group can be as long as forty-five minutes, depending on your group size and what you feel comfortable with.

Why two crafts? We have chosen to include two crafts to provide variety for the programmer. You may feel that one craft suits your group better than the other, or you may be looking for something new to try. Whatever the case, each craft provided has been tested and approved by children we have worked with over the past few years, and you can't ask for a better endorsement than that!

Fours and Fives: Pumpkin Patch

Just because these songs and rhymes are associated with autumn does not mean that you have to wait until the fall to use them. Why not include this in a week or month of using the four seasons as a unit? There are so many great songs and rhymes surrounding fall that doing this topic twice a year will only begin to touch the resources available to cover it. We believe we've given you the best. Jump in!

Books to Share

The Scarecrow's Hat by Ken Brown

Once Upon a Golden Apple by Jean Little, Maggie DeVries, and Phoebe Gilman

How to Make an Apple Pie and See the World by Marjorie Priceman

Pumpkin Soup by Helen Cooper

Too Many Pumpkins by Linda White

The Pumpkin Book by Gail Gibbons

Awesome Activity

If the leaves have started falling when your program is scheduled, have the children bring in a few leaves each from their gardens or a nearby park. Collect some extras yourself for those children who may forget. If the leaves haven't hit the ground in your area yet, or if you are lucky enough to live in the land of palm trees, cut out a variety of leaves from construction paper. Make sure each child in your group has two or three leaves. Using a simple book with bold pictures (such as *Autumn Leaves* by Ken Robbins), have children match their leaves to the ones displayed in the book. Once you have identified all the leaves, explain to the children that it is time to gather them up for mulching! Have each child put his or her leaves in a clear plastic bag as you sing (to the tune of "Farmer in the Dell") :

We're gathering up the leaves,
We're gathering up the leaves,
High-ho it's fall you know,
And we're gathering up the leaves.

(Repeat as often as you need to until you get all of the leaves into the bag.)

From Beth Maddigan and Stefanie Drennan, *The BIG Book of Reading, Rhyming, and Resources: Programs for Children Ages 4-8*. Westport, CT: Libraries Unlimited. © 2005.

Fours and Fives: Pumpkin Patch

Rhymes and Songs

Pumpkin Poem

(Suit actions to words.)

> One day I found two pumpkin seeds,
> I planted one and pulled the weeds.
> It sprouted roots and a big long vine,
> A pumpkin grew; I called it mine.
> The pumpkin was quite round and fat,
> (I really am quite proud of that.)
> But there is something I'll admit,
> That has me worried just a bit.
> I ate the other seed you see,
> Now . . . will it grow inside of me?

(Let the children answer . . .)

> I'm so relieved since I have found,
> That pumpkins only grow in the ground.

Scarecrow, Scarecrow

(Tune: Teddy Bear, Teddy Bear)
(Suit actions to words.)

> Scarecrow, scarecrow, turn around,
> Scarecrow, scarecrow, jump up and down.
> Scarecrow, scarecrow, raise your arms
>   high,
> Scarecrow, scarecrow, wink one eye.
> Scarecrow, scarecrow, bend your knees,
> Scarecrow, scarecrow, flap in the breeze.
> Scarecrow, scarecrow, climb into bed,
> Scarecrow, scarecrow, rest your head.

Dingle Dangle Scarecrow

(Suit actions to words.)

> When all the cows were sleeping
> And the sun had gone to bed,
> Up jumped the scarecrow

(Jump up.)

> And this is what he said!
> I'm a dingle dangle scarecrow
> With a flippy floppy hat.

> I can shake my hands like this,
> I can shake my feet like that!

(Sit down.)

> When all the hens were roosting
> And the moon's behind the cloud,
> Up jumped the scarecrow,

(Jump up.)

> And shouted very loud.
> I'm a dingle dangle scarecrow
> With a flippy, floppy hat.
> I can shake my hands like this,
> I can shake my feet like that!

(Sit down.)

> When the dogs were in the kennels
> And the doves were in the loft,
> Up jumped the scarecrow

(Jump up.)

> And whispered very soft,
> I'm a dingle dangle scarecrow,
> With a flippy, floppy hat.
> I can shake my hands like this,
> I can shake my feet like that!
> I'm a dingle dangle scarecrow
> With a flippy floppy hat.
> I can shake my hands like this,
> I can shake my feet like that!

(Sit down.)

I'm a Little Scarecrow

(Tune: I'm a Little Teapot)
(Suit actions to words.)

> I'm a little scarecrow,
> Raggedy and worn.
> I wear a hat
> And a shirt that is torn.
> When the crows come
> I wave and shout,
> "Away from my garden,
> Go on, get out!"

From Beth Maddigan and Stefanie Drennan, *The BIG Book of Reading, Rhyming, and Resources: Programs for Children Ages 4-8*. Westport, CT: Libraries Unlimited. © 2005.

Fours and Fives: Pumpkin Patch

Floppy Scarecrow

(Suit actions to words.)
(Have the children stand for this rhyme.)

The floppy, floppy scarecrow
Guards his field all day.
He waves his floppy, floppy hands
To scare the crows away!
(Replace hands with arms, head, legs etc.)

Ten Red Apples

(Suit actions to words.)

Ten red apples growing on a tree,

(Hold hands up high.)

Five for you and five for me.

(Shake one hand, then the other.)

Help me shake the tree just so,

(Shake whole body.)

And ten red apples will fall down below.

(Lower hands while fluttering fingers.)

One, two, three, four, five.

(Count fingers on one hand.)

Six, seven, eight, nine, ten.

(Count fingers on opposite hand.)

Autumn Leaves

(Start with the children standing in a circle.)

Autumn leaves are hanging,
Hanging, hanging,
Autumn leaves are hanging,
All day long.
(Stand with arms outstretched.)

Additional verses:
Autumn leaves are turning colours—*(Turn around.)*
Autumn leaves are falling down—*(Lower self to the floor.)*
Autumn leaves are dancing—*(Dance on the spot.)*
Autumn leaves are being raked—*(Children gather together.)*

Five Leaves

(Tune: Six Little Ducks)
(Use your fingers to represent the leaves.)

Five little leaves so bright and gay,
Were dancing about on a tree one day.
The wind came blowing through the town,
And one little leaf came tumbling down.
4, 3, 2, 1

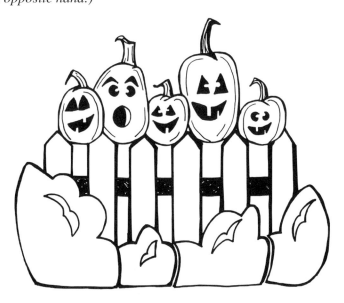

From Beth Maddigan and Stefanie Drennan, *The BIG Book of Reading, Rhyming, and Resources: Programs for Children Ages 4-8*. Westport, CT: Libraries Unlimited. © 2005.

Fours and Fives: Pumpkin Patch

Candy Apple

Handy Hint 1—This craft should be done at the beginning of your program to allow the paint to dry.

Handy Hint 2—Be sure to cover your tables with butcher paper or plastic drop cloths, as this craft is very sticky!

Materials

1 medium Styrofoam™ ball per child

Red washable tempera paint

White glue

Red glitter

1 craft stick per child

Paintbrushes

Waxed paper

Instructions

1. To begin, cut one piece of waxed paper, 4-by-4-inch or 10-by-10 cm, per child.

2. Mix together the red paint and the white glue. The portions should be two-thirds paint to one-third glue.

3. Cut a small piece off the bottom of the Styrofoam ball so that it sits flat.

4. Insert the craft stick into the top of the ball.

5. Lay the waxed paper squares around your craft table so that each child has a square in front of him or her.

6. Provide the children with paintbrushes and let them paint the entire surface of the Styrofoam.

7. Once the surface is painted, let the children finish the craft by sprinkling red glitter on their apple and letting it dry.

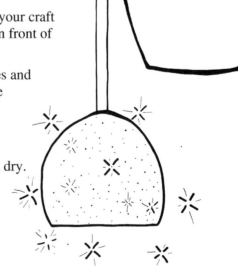

Fours and Fives: Pumpkin Patch

Apple-icious!

Handy Hint—Have children carry their crafts home flat. If the glue hasn't had enough time to dry, the pieces may end up on the floor, causing tears for some very unhappy children.

Materials

Brown paper lunch bags—1 per child

Popsicle™ sticks—6 per child

Red/yellow/brown construction paper, felt or patterned/textured paper of any kind, to make 2 apples per child

4 small buttons per child

Yarn

Hole punch

Glue sticks—1 per child

Scissors/pinking shears

Instructions

1. Photocopy (and enlarge) the Apple-icious! banner and cut out one per child. (Pinking shears create a nice effect!)

2. Using the apple template (enlarged), trace the apples onto whatever material you choose to use, then cut them out.

3. Cut a length of yarn approximately 12 inches or 30 cm long.

4. Lay the paper bag lengthwise in front of you and punch two holes in the top left and right corners of the bag. Tie the ends of the string through the holes on either end. This is what you will use to hang the craft.

Fours and Fives: Pumpkin Patch

5. Glue the edges and the end of the paper bag together so that the flaps don't pop open and the bag stays closed.

6. Glue Popsicle sticks around the outer edge—this should look like a frame.

7. Glue the two apples in the centre of the bag.

8. Finally, glue two buttons onto the centre of each apple (these will look like the seeds in the middle of the apple) and glue the Apple-icious! banner near the top centre of the bag.

Fours and Fives: Hallowe'en Hoedown

'Tis the season to be slimy! Hallowe'en marks the beginning of the holiday season for children, and could there be any better way to begin the celebrations? Planning a costume party for your group is easier than you may think and will require little preparation on your part. You may want to type a small note to hand out to parents and/or caregivers at registration time to let them know what date you'll be having your party and also to make any patrons who do not partake in Hallowe'en aware of what you are planning. Some of the songs in this chapter borrow their tunes from more traditional favourites (e.g., "We Three Ghosts" from "We Three Kings"), and this also may bother some patrons. It is important in your planning to remember to be sensitive to the different ethnicities and cultures in your community. Having the children wear costumes should be optional, as some parents/caregivers may not want to dress their children up more than once, and some families may not celebrate Hallowe'en.

Note: Remember to remind everyone a week or two in advance of the party.

Books to Share

The Runaway Pumpkin by Kevin Lewis

The Little Old Lady Who Was Not Afraid of Anything by Linda Williams

Mouse's First Hallowe'en by Lauren Thompson

Shake Dem Hallowe'en Bones by W. Nikola-Lisa

Big Pumpkin by Erica Silverman

Rattlebone Rock by Sylvia Andrews

Great Game

Pin the Tail on the Cat

Getting started: Here's a new spin on an old favourite. Enlarge and make a photocopy of the cat template provided or draw one on black construction paper, using white chalk, and cut it out. Laminate the cat if possible using a laminator or clear, sticky contact paper. This will ensure that you get more than one use out of the game. Using the cat tail template, cut out and laminate several cat tails to "pin" on the cat (enough for one per child in your group). Using masking tape, place several pieces of tape on the back of the cat and adhere it to a wall (at child level) somewhere close to where you will be having your party. Keep the tape handy, as you will need it to "pin" the tail on the cat.

When you are ready to play: (You can either use a scarf to blindfold the players or simply have them close their eyes.) Begin by spinning each child around three times slowly and, once you have attached a small piece of tape to the back of the tail, give it to each child as he or she is ready to "pin" the tail on the cat. Remove the blindfold or have the child open his or her eyes once the tail has been stuck to the cat. The game is over when each child has had a turn.

From Beth Maddigan and Stefanie Drennan, *The BIG Book of Reading, Rhyming, and Resources: Programs for Children Ages 4-8*. Westport, CT: Libraries Unlimited. © 2005.

Fours and Fives: Hallowe'en Hoedown

The Very Popular Skeleton Dance

By Michele Hopkins

Have the children stand, and make sure they have enough room to move without bumping into anyone. Once this is done, begin by instructing the children to do the following:

First let your wrists move (*Loosen and turn wrists.*)
Now let your elbows go (*Let your elbows join in.*)
And now your whole arm (*Let your whole arm go limp.*)

Now let's try our legs . . .
First one leg (*Lift one leg and shake it about loosely.*)
And then the other leg (*Repeat with other leg.*)
And then both! (*Shake both legs loosely.*)

Next let your head go (*Move your head back and forth and up and down.*)
Your shoulders (*Loosen your shoulders.*)
And hips (*Wiggle your hips.*)

Now all together let's dance! (*Programmer chants:*)

Skeletons dancing all around,
Skeletons dancing up and down.
Skeletons dancing with delight,
Skeletons dancing through the night.

HUSH . . . pause (*Put your fingers to your lips and say shhhhh . . . while you crouch down low.*)

Jump up! Jump down! (*Jump up and then crumple to the ground in a pile of bones.*)

> ***Fun Factor***—Repeat approximately three times. The last time, get everyone to fall into a bag of bones (*a crumpled up skeleton on the floor*) and hold that pose for a few seconds.

Fours and Fives: Hallowe'en Hoedown

Pumpkin Bells

(Tune: Jingle Bells)
(Suit actions to words.)
(Break out the bells for this song!)

Dashing through the streets,
In our costumes bright as day!
To each house we go,
Laughing all the way . . .
BOO! BOO! BOO!
Hallowe'en is here,
Making spirits bright,
What fun it is to trick or treat
And sing some songs tonight.
Oh . . .
Pumpkin bells, pumpkin bells,
Ringing loud and clear.
Oh what fun Great Pumpkin brings
When Hallowe'en is here.
Oh . . .
Pumpkin bells, pumpkin bells,
Ringing loud and clear.
Oh what fun Great Pumpkin brings,
When Hallowe'en is here.

This Old Ghost

(Tune: This Old Man)

This old ghost, he played one,
He played peek-a-boo on the run.

(Cover your eyes with your hands.)

With a Boo! Boo! Boo!
And a Clap! Clap! Clap!

(Clap your hands.)

This old ghost is a friendly chap.

This old ghost, he played two,
He'll play peek-a-boo with you.

(Cover your eyes with your hands.)

With a Boo! Boo! Boo!
And a Clap! Clap! Clap!

(Clap your hands.)

This old ghost is a friendly chap.

This old ghost, he played three,
He played peek-a-boo with me.

(Cover your eyes with your hands.)

With a Boo! Boo! Boo!
And a Clap! Clap! Clap!

(Clap your hands.)

This old ghost is a friendly chap.

Six Little Ghosts

(Tune: Six Little Ducks)

Six little ghosts that I once knew,
Spooky ones, kooky ones, shy ones too.
But the one little ghost had a special job to do . . .
He led the others with a Boo! Boo! Boo!
Boo! Boo! Boo!
Boo! Boo! Boo!
He led the others with a Boo! Boo! Boo!

Down to the haunted house they flew,
In and out, round about, through and through.
But the one little ghost had a special job to do,
He led the others with a Boo! Boo! Boo!
Boo! Boo! Boo!
Boo! Boo! Boo!
He led the others with a Boo! Boo! Boo!

Hallowe'en Sounds

(Tune: London Bridge)

This is the way the witches fly,
Witches fly, witches fly.
This is the way the witches fly,
Swish! Swish! Swish!

Additional verses:

This is the way the ghosts go by—Boo!
  Boo! Boo!
This is the way the night owls cry—Hoo,
  hoo, hoo
This is the way the pumpkins laugh—Hee!
  Hee! Hee!
This is the sound the black bats
  make—Eee! Eee! Eee!

From Beth Maddigan and Stefanie Drennan, *The BIG Book of Reading, Rhyming, and Resources: Programs for Children Ages 4-8*. Westport, CT: Libraries Unlimited. © 2005.

Fours and Fives: Hallowe'en Hoedown

We Three Ghosts

(Tune: We Three Kings)

We three ghosts of Hallowe'en are
Scaring kids who wander too far.
Trick or treating, candy eating,
Watching for the Hallowe'en Star.
Oh . . . oh . . .
Star of darkness, star of night,
Star of every gruesome sight.
West winds howling, cat's a-yowling,
Let us play some tricks tonight.

Deck the Halls with Poison Ivy

(Tune: Deck the Halls)

Deck the halls with poison ivy,
Fa la la la la la la la la.
'Tis the season to be slimy,
Fa la la la la la la la la.
Don we now our strange apparel,
Fa la la, la la la, la la la.
Troll the ancient Hallowe'en carol,
Fa la la la la, la la la la.

See the goblins rise before us,
Fa la la la la la la la la.
As we sing the Hallowe'en chorus,
Fa la la la la la la la la.
Follow them as they ascend,
Fa la la, la la la, la la la.
To join with all their spooky friends,
Fa la la la la, la la la la.

Hallowe'en Is Coming Soon

(Tune: London Bridge)

Hallowe'en is coming soon,
Coming soon, coming soon.
Hallowe'en is coming soon,
Oh, what fun!

Additional verses:

Owl's a-hooting in the trees—Whoo!
   Whoo! Whoo!
Ghosts are flying through the air—Boo!
   Boo! Boo!

Witches flying on their brooms—Eee!
   Eee! Eee!
Jack-o'-lanterns grin at you—Hee! Hee! Hee!

Hallowe'en is coming soon,
Coming soon, coming soon.
Hallowe'en is coming soon,
Oh, what fun!

What Witches Do

(Use your fingers to represent the witches in this fingerplay. Every time you say the words "The witches," wiggle your fingers up and down and then follow along, suiting your actions to the words.)

The witches don their pointed hats,

(Wiggle fingers, then pretend to put on a hat.)

The witches croak and croon.

(Wiggle fingers.)

The witches ride their broomsticks,

(Wiggle fingers.)

Away beyond the moon.

(Point to the sky.)

The witches don their flowing cloaks,

(Wiggle your fingers, then flap your arms behind you.)

The witches stir their brew.

(Wiggle your fingers, then pretend to stir a cauldron.)

The witches chant their magic spells,

(Wiggle fingers.)

All the dark hours though.

The witches stroke the big black cats,

(Wiggle your fingers, then pretend to pet a cat.)

They comb their locks of gray.

(Pretend to brush your hair with your fingers.)

Yet when a hint of daylight comes . . .
   (Pause.)

The witches hide away!

(Say the last line quickly and hide your fingers behind your back.)

From Beth Maddigan and Stefanie Drennan, *The BIG Book of Reading, Rhyming, and Resources: Programs for Children Ages 4-8*. Westport, CT: Libraries Unlimited. © 2005.

Fours and Fives: Hallowe'en Hoedown

Crafty Creation

A-Door-Able Hallowe'en Wreath

Handy Hint—*If you use a photocopier to reproduce the Hallowe'en picture templates, once you have them copied, staple four or five sheets together and then cut them out. This will save time and get the cutting done more quickly!*

Materials

Paper plates—1 per child

Photocopy paper—various colours

Scissors

Yarn

Hole punch

Glue sticks—1 per child

Decorating materials—markers, crayons, glitter

Instructions

1. Trace or photocopy (and enlarge) the Hallowe'en picture templates provided on various colours of photocopy paper and cut them out.

2. Cut out the inside circle of the paper plate and discard it. The outside rim will be your wreath.

3. Cut a length of yarn approximately 6 inches or 15 cm in length.

4. Using the hole punch, punch a hole in the top of the wreath and tie the yarn on so that you have a loop to hang the wreath with.

5. Last, glue the Hallowe'en pictures around the wreath, colour them with markers and/or accent with them glitter, then simply hang them on your door and enjoy!

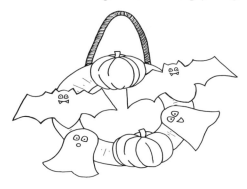

From Beth Maddigan and Stefanie Drennan, *The BIG Book of Reading, Rhyming, and Resources: Programs for Children Ages 4-8*. Westport, CT: Libraries Unlimited. © 2005.

Fours and Fives: Hallowe'en Hoedown

Fours and Fives: Hallowe'en Hoedown

Crafty Creation

Black Cat Mask-erade!

Handy Hint—*Paint the plates black ahead of time to cut down on time in the craft portion of your program.*

Materials

Sturdy paper plates—1 plate for every 2 children

Paint sticks—1 per child

Black pipe cleaners—2 per child

Pink construction paper

Black construction paper

Black tempera paint

Exacto™ knife—This should only be used by the programmer/adult in the program and should be kept well out of the reach of children.

Instructions

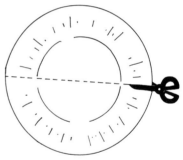

1. Cut the paper plate in half; trace two eyes onto the plate; and using an Exacto knife, cut the eyes out along the drawn lines. (If you choose to paint the plates in advance, this should be your next step.)

2. Using masking tape, tape a paint stick to the right or left side of each plate (this will be the handle of the mask).

3. Cut each black pipe cleaner into three pieces and glue three whiskers onto each side of the cat's face.

4. Cut out two ears from black construction paper. Glue these onto either side of the cat's face.

5. Cut out a triangle 2-by-2-by-2-inch or 5-by-5-by-5 cm in size from the pink construction paper. Glue it (with one of the three points pointed at you) in the middle of the bottom part of the plate. (See diagram.) This is your cat's nose.

Fours and Fives: Hallowe'en Hoedown

Fours and Fives: Underwater Adventure

Sea creatures, flippers, and fins—oh my! Dive into the underwater world and you're sure to meet with some giggles and laughter. Children seem to be fascinated by the things that live in the ocean, perhaps because in their eyes there is so much that cannot be explained. How do they breathe? Where do they sleep? What do they eat? Where are their mommies and daddies? These are all questions that you as the programmer should take the time to research and try to have answers for. Four and five year olds are just as curious as they were when they were two. The difference is that now they are better able to understand the answers and explanations that we as programmers and teachers can provide.

Books to Share

A Swim Through the Sea by Kristin Joy Pratt

Stella, Star of the Sea by Marie-Louise Gay

In the Ocean by Maurice Pledger

Smiley Shark by Ruth Galloway

Fidgety Fish by Ruth Galloway

Somewhere in the Ocean by Jennifer Ward

Great Game

Gone Fishing

Getting started—Your group will have a whale of a time with this fun game! Start by drawing the outlines of various fish (sharks, whales, swordfish, minnows) onto coloured construction paper and cut them out. Laminate them or use clear plastic contact paper to make them sturdier. Next, attach a piece of magnet strip onto one side of each fish and set them aside. Use child-sized fishing rods with magnets on the ends (you can find these at your local dollar or discount store) to pretend to fish. As an alternative, attach a paper clip to one end of a piece of string and attach the other end to a ruler or piece of doweling for a handle.

When you are ready to play: Put all of the fish into a large bucket or tub and set it in the middle of your circle. Divide the children into groups or play individually. The game is over when all of the fish have been caught.

> *Fun Factor*—Sing the "Off I Go A-Fishing" song as you play. Or, to make this game more challenging, before laminating your fish, you could add a trivia question (True or False—crabs walk sideways?) or music challenge (sing "Row, Row, Row Your Boat") to each fish. If you divide your group into teams, another alternative would be to assign a point value to each fish along with the challenge (two points for a correct answer, one point for trying). It's very easy to adapt this game to whatever theme or unit you are studying or focusing on. By the way, the answer to the trivia question is *true*. Happy Fishing!

From Beth Maddigan and Stefanie Drennan, *The BIG Book of Reading, Rhyming, and Resources: Programs for Children Ages 4-8*. Westport, CT: Libraries Unlimited. © 2005.

Fours and Fives: Underwater Adventure

Rhymes and Songs

At the Seashore

(Suit actions to words.)

Down at the seashore
Isn't it grand?
Wiggling my toes
In the soft warm sand.

Building a tall sand castle
Where the king and queen can stay.
But when the tide comes rushing in,
They'll have to move away.

Splashing in the water
Of the cool blue sea.
Playing wave tag in and out,
You can't catch me!

Holding up a seashell,
Tightly to my ear.
Shh! It's telling me a secret,
That only I can hear.

Five Little Frogs

(Recite the poem below and let the children fill in the blanks at the end using whatever object, animal, or mammal they choose, no matter how silly.)

5 little frogs
Were down at the pond,
Down at the pond at play.
Along came a hungry _____,
And chased one frog away.

4 little frogs
Were down at the pond,
Down at the pond at play.
Along came a wiggly _____,
And chased one frog away.

3 little frogs
Were down at the pond,
Down at the pond at play.
Along came a giant _____,

And chased one frog away.
2 little frogs
Were down at the pond,
Down at the pond at play.
Along came a purple _____,
And chased one frog away.

1 little frog
Was down at the pond,
Down at the pond at play.
Along came a flying _____,
And chased one frog away.

Then no little frogs
Were down at the pond,
Down at the pond at play.
Where do you think the little frogs went,
When they all hopped away?

The Sharks in the Sea

(Tune: The Wheels on the Bus)

(Make up your own actions for this fun song or ask the children to give you their ideas.)

The sharks in the sea go
Chomp, chomp, chomp,
Chomp, chomp, chomp,
Chomp, chomp, chomp.
The sharks in the sea go,
Chomp, chomp, chomp,
All day long.

Additional verses:

Fish in the sea—swim, swim, swim
Lobsters in the sea—pinch, pinch, pinch
Octopus in the sea—wiggle, wiggle, wiggle
Sea horse in the sea—rocks back and forth
Whale in the sea—squirt, squirt, squirt
Clam in the sea—open and shut
Crabs in the sea—click, click, click
Jellyfish in the sea—bloop, bloop, bloop

From Beth Maddigan and Stefanie Drennan, *The BIG Book of Reading, Rhyming, and Resources: Programs for Children Ages 4-8*. Westport, CT: Libraries Unlimited. © 2005.

Fours and Fives: Underwater Adventure

Seashell

(This poem would be a good quieting routine to start your group or circle time.)

One day a little shell washed up

(Pretend to hold a shell.)

Out of the waves at sea.
I held the shell up to my ear,

(Pretend to hold a shell to your ear.)

And I heard it sing to me.
Shh . . . shh . . . shh . . . shh.

(Have the children repeat shh sound.)

A little shell washed up one day,
And lay upon the sand.

(Pretend to hold a shell in your hand.)

It sang a song about the sea,
As I held it in my hand.
Shh . . . shh . . . shh . . . shh.

5 Little Sea Creatures

(Use your fingers to represent the sea creatures.)

5 little sea creatures
On the ocean floor.
The lobster walked away,
Now there are 4.

4 little sea creatures
Living in the sea.
The octopus crept away,
Now there are 3.

3 little sea creatures
Wondering what to do.
"Good-bye," said the starfish,
Now there are 2.

2 little sea creatures
Not having much fun.
Off swam the sea horse,
Now there is 1.

1 little hermit crab
Sad and all alone.
Back came the starfish,

Back came the sea horse,
Back came the octopus,
Back came the lobster
Then all 5 went home.

I Went to the Beach

(Cut out, photocopy, or draw pictures to accompany this rhyme ahead of time. Hold the pictures up as you say each verse.)

I went to the beach
And what did I see?
A bird on the sand
Looking at me!

I went to the beach
And what did I see?
A fish in the water
Splashing at me!

I went to the beach
And what did I see?
A shell in the sand
Sparkling at me!

I went to the beach
And what did I see?
A crab in its shell
Waving at me!

5 Little Seashells

(Use your fingers to represent the seashells in this poem or draw seashells onto coloured construction paper, cut them out, and laminate them.)

5 little seashells lying on the shore,
Swish! went the waves and then there were 4.
4 little seashells as cozy as could be,
Swish! went the waves and then there were 3.
3 little seashells all pearly and new,
Swish! went the waves and then there were 2.
2 little seashells sleeping in the sun,
Swish! went the waves and then there was 1.
1 little seashell left all alone,
Whispered "Shhhh" as I took it home.

From Beth Maddigan and Stefanie Drennan, *The BIG Book of Reading, Rhyming, and Resources: Programs for Children Ages 4-8*. Westport, CT: Libraries Unlimited. © 2005.

Fours and Fives: Underwater Adventure

Off I Go A-Fishing

(Tune: The More We Get Together)
(Suit actions to words.)

Off I go a-fishing, a-fishing, a-fishing,
Off I go a-fishing,
To the sparkling brook.

(Pretend to swing a fishing pole over your shoulder.)

I hope there is a big one, a big one, a big
one,
I hope there is a big one,
To nibble on my hook.

(Hold your hands out in front of you to show how big your fish will be.)

First I cast my line in, my line in, my line
in,
First I cast my line in,
And hold the pole so tight.

(Pretend to cast off.)

Watch the bobber go under, go under, go
under,
Watch the bobber go under,
I think I've got a bite!

(Nod your head up and down when the bobber goes under.)

Now I start a-reeling, a-reeling, a-reeling,
Now I start a-reeling,
This fish must weigh a lot.

(Pretend to be reeling in a big fish.)

Here it comes a-wriggling, a-wriggling,
a-wriggling,
Here it comes a-wriggling,
Just see what I have caught!

(Pretend to be holding up a huge fish.)

From Beth Maddigan and Stefanie Drennan, *The BIG Book of Reading, Rhyming, and Resources: Programs for Children Ages 4-8*. Westport, CT: Libraries Unlimited. © 2005.

Fours and Fives: Underwater Adventure

Crafty Creation

Finally a use for those pesky CDs we get in the mail!

Handy Hint—*Ask friends, parents, and co-workers to save the CDs they get in the mail for you. You'll be surprised at how quickly they will add up!*

Flashy Fish

Materials

2 CDs per child

White glue

Construction paper—any colour

Decorating materials—chunky glitter, stickers

Glue sticks

Instructions

1. Glue two CDs together (shiny side out) and let dry.

2. Photocopy (and enlarge) and then trace the fin and tail templates onto construction paper and cut them out.

3. Glue the fins and tail onto the CDs (see diagram of finished product).

4. Let the children decorate their fish with glitter, stickers, etc., using glue sticks.

From Beth Maddigan and Stefanie Drennan, *The BIG Book of Reading, Rhyming, and Resources: Programs for Children Ages 4-8*. Westport, CT: Libraries Unlimited. © 2005.

Fours and Fives: Underwater Adventure

Fours and Fives: Underwater Adventure

Crafty Creation

Under-the-Sea Star

Handy Hint—If you plan on dying the barley, do it a week ahead of time to allow for drying. This also allows you to have your program ready if someone needs to cover for you in case of illness.

Materials

Construction paper—various colors

Baby barley or sand

Red and yellow food colouring

Rubbing alcohol

Scissors

Glue—white or stick

Instructions

1. Combine the red and yellow food coloring to make orange an two caps full of rubbing alcohol.

2. Add baby barley to the mixture and leave it in long enough fc the colour to adhere (approximately ten to fifteen minutes).

3. Once you have your desired shade, let the baby barley dry on a paper towel.

4. Photocopy (and enlarge), trace onto different colors of construction paper, and cut out the sea star template (enough for your group).

5. Glue the baby barley to the sea star and let it dry.

From Beth Maddigan and Stefanie Drennan, *The BIG Book of Reading, Rhyming, and Resources: Programs for Children Ages 4-8*. Westport, CT: Libraries Unlimited. © 2005.

Fours and Fives: Creepy Crawlies

They love them or they hate them. Squish them or squash them. Could sit for hours and watch them. They're creepy crawlies. Creepy crawlies is another program to help foster your group's sense of curiosity. The Itsy Bitsy Spider Crafty Creation is interactive and fun. The children will want to use it over and over again. You never know, this program may even help the children who are afraid of bugs realize that they can be fascinating.

Books to Share

The Bugliest Bug by Carol Diggery Shields

Because a Little Bug Went Kachoo! by Rosetta Stone

Bugs! Bugs! Bugs! by Bob Barner

Quick As a Cricket by Audrey Wood

The Big Bug Ball by Dee Lilligard

Bugs! by David T. Greenburg

Awesome Activity

Flea, Fly Mosquito

You may remember singing this song when you were young. It's a lot of fun and will get your whole group involved, so much so that they will ask you to sing it again and again! Sit with your group in a circle and ask them to repeat after you when you sing the following:

Flea! *(Repeat.)*

Flea, fly! *(Repeat.)*

Flea, fly, mosquito! *(Repeat.)*

Ooooh no-no, no more mosquitoes! (Repeat.)

Itchy-itchy, scratchy- scratchy, ooh I got one down my back-y! *(Repeat.)*

(Pretend to be bitten by a mosquito.)

Beat that big bad bug with bug spray! *(Repeat.)*

Shhhhhhhhhhhhhhhh! (repeat)

(Pretend to be spraying the bugs.)

> *Fun Factor*—Once your group has gotten the hang of this song, try singing it at different voice levels (softly, normal, loudly, etc.).

From Beth Maddigan and Stefanie Drennan, *The BIG Book of Reading, Rhyming, and Resources: Programs for Children Ages 4-8*. Westport, CT: Libraries Unlimited. © 2005.

Fours and Fives: Creepy Crawlies

Rhymes and Songs

The Moving Song

(Tune: Jingle Bells)
(Suit actions to words.)

> Clap your hands, stomp your feet,
> Wiggle all around.
> Reach your hands high in the air,
> And now let's touch the ground.
> Shake your head, wiggle your arms,
> Give yourself a hug.
> Lay down flat upon the ground,
> But watch out for the BUGS!

Spiders

(Tune: Six Little Ducks)
(Use your fingers to represent the spiders.)

> 5 little spiders in a web,
> 5 little spiders ready for bed.
> Down came the rain and it rained all day,
> And 1 little spider crawled away.
>
> 4, 3, 2, 1

I Have a Little Spider

(Tune: Miss Lucy Had a Baby)
(Use your hand to represent the spider.)

> I have a little spider,
> I'm very fond of him.
> He climbs on to my shoulder,

(Make your hand crawl to your shoulder.)

> And then up to my chin.

(Make your hand crawl to your chin.)

> He crawls straight down my arm,

(Make your hand crawl down your arm.)

> And right to my leg.

(Make your hand crawl down your leg.)

> But now he's a tired spider,
> So I put him straight to bed!

(Pretend to fall asleep.)

Little Red Bug

(Cut a large red circle out of felt, add two wiggle eyes at the top along with a pipe cleaner, cut in half and taped on for the antennae. Also cut out five black felt circles for the spots.)

> Little red bug, oh so cute,
> Here's a black spot for your suit.
> Now you go and have some fun,
> With your spot, your very first one.
>
> Little red bug, oh so cute,
> Here's a black spot for your suit.
> It's so nice to own a few,
> So enjoy these lovely two.
>
> Little red bug, oh so cute,
> Here's a black spot for your suit.
> We are very pleased to see,
> How nice you look wearing all three.
>
> Little red bug, oh so cute,
> Here's a black spot for your suit.
> You might feel that you need more,
> So we'll happily give your four.
>
> Little red bug, oh so cute,
> Here's a black spot for your suit.
> Heavens, heavens, sakes alive,
> Look at you, you're wearing five!

From Beth Maddigan and Stefanie Drennan, *The BIG Book of Reading, Rhyming, and Resources: Programs for Children Ages 4-8*. Westport, CT: Libraries Unlimited. © 2005.

Fours and Fives: Creepy Crawlies

Creepy Crawlies

(Tune: Sleeping Bunnies)
(Just like the sleeping bunnies, have the children pretend to be each of the creepy crawly critters in this song. Start by having the children pretend to be asleep on the floor.)

See the little spiders sleeping
Till it's nearly noon.
Come and let us gently wake them,
With this merry tune.
Oh how still . . .
Are they ill?
WAKE UP SOON!

Crawl little spiders, crawling, crawling,
Crawl little spiders, crawl, crawl, crawl.
Crawl little spiders, crawling, crawling,
Crawl little spiders, crawl and fall!

(Fall to the floor)

Additional verses:

Caterpillars—spinning
Bumblebees—buzzing
Butterflies—floating
Ladybugs—flying

The Spider in the Web

(Tune: The Farmer in the Dell)

The spider in the web,

(Make a spider with your fingers.)

The spider in the web,
Spin, spin, oh watch him spin,
The spider in the web.

The spider eats a bug—eeew!

(Say "eeew" louder each time.)

The spider eats a bug—eeew!
Crunch, crunch, munch, munch,
The spider eats a bug—eeew!

The spider falls asleep—snore!

(Pretend to sleep.)

The spider falls asleep—snore!
Dreaming of the bugs he eats,
The spider falls asleep—snore!

Little Spider

(Tune: Itsy Bitsy Spider)
(Use your fingers to form a spider to illustrate the actions in this song.)

See the little spider
Climbing up the wall.

(Creep fingers up child's arm.)

See the little spider
Stumble and then fall.

(Move fingers quickly down child's arm.)

See the little spider
Tumble down the street.

(Move fingers down child's leg.)

See the little spider
Stop down at my feet.

(Stop fingers at child's feet.)

I'm a Little Spider

(Tune: I'm a Little Teapot)
(Use your fingers to form a spider to illustrate this song.)

I'm a little spider
Watch me spin.
If you'll be my dinner
I'll let you come in.
Then I'll build my web
And hold you tight.
And gobble you up
In one BIG BITE!

From Beth Maddigan and Stefanie Drennan, *The BIG Book of Reading, Rhyming, and Resources: Programs for Children Ages 4-8*. Westport, CT: Libraries Unlimited. © 2005.

Fours and Fives: Creepy Crawlies

Crafty Creation

Itsy Bitsy Spider

You can make this itsy bitsy spider climb up his very own waterspout. This craft requires most of the prep work to be done ahead of time.

Handy Hint 1—To cut down on your workload, you could cut the aluminium foil into squares and make it a part of the decorating materials that the children will use at the end of the program.

Handy Hint 2—Ask parents/caregivers and co-workers to help you collect the paper towel rolls that you will need. They will add up very quickly.

Materials

Paper towel rolls—enough for your group

Aluminium foil

Black pom-poms (medium sized—to fit through the paper towel roll)—enough for your group

Black yarn

Wiggle eyes—small

Glue sticks

Scissors

Decorating materials—markers, crayons, glitter

Instructions

1. Cover the paper towel rolls with aluminium foil and set aside. (These are the waterspouts and they are finished until the children decorate them.)

2. Cut a length of string approximately 2 inches/5 cm longer than the paper towel roll. Attach one end of the string to the pom-pom (by tying it around the middle) and knot it. Be sure to leave ½-inch/1.5 cm of string so that you can tie both ends together later.

3. To make the spider, cut eight small strips of black construction paper and glue them onto the pom-pom, four on each side. (These are the spiders' legs.) Glue on the wiggle eyes.

4. Feed one end of the string through the paper towel roll and bring it out the other end. Tie the ends of the string together. (This should form a loop through the roll that, when you pull on the string, will make it look as though the spider is crawling up the waterspout.)

5. Let the children decorate the water pipe.

Fours and Fives: Creepy Crawlies

Crafty Creation

Lovely Ladybug Puppet Pal

Simple, pretty, and not too creepy, this ladybug will be a hit with your little crafters!

Materials

Large paper plates—2 per child

Scissors

Stapler

Red and black paint, markers or crayons

Glue sticks

Black construction paper

Black or red pipe cleaners—1 per child

Hole punch

Large wiggle eyes—optional

Instructions

1. Using the template, photocopy (enlarge as needed to fit), trace, and cut out two sets of ladybug legs (from black construction paper) for each ladybug.

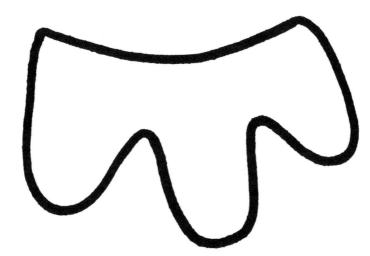

2. Staple or tape two paper plates together, leaving one end of the ladybug unstapled (a hole large enough to put a hand in) by putting the eating surfaces of the plates on the inside. Make sure to staple the legs in between the two plates (see illustration of the final craft).

Fours and Fives: Creepy Crawlies

3. Cut off the bottom portion of the plates (where they were not stapled or taped). This is where you will put your hand to move the ladybug.

4. Have the children paint or colour the top of the ladybug red (except the head, which should be painted or coloured black).

5. Next, paint on some black dots or glue some black circles on its back, then either paint on eyes or glue on wiggle eyes.

6. Punch two holes at the top of the ladybug for the antennae. Cut a pipe cleaner in half, thread one-half through the first hole, and twist the ends together (so it doesn't fall out), and do the same with the second half of the pipe cleaner.

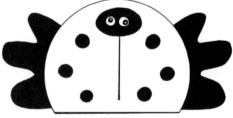

From Beth Maddigan and Stefanie Drennan, *The BIG Book of Reading, Rhyming, and Resources: Programs for Children Ages 4-8*. Westport, CT: Libraries Unlimited. © 2005.

Fours and Fives: Fairy Folk

If you have ever wondered what it feels like to fly, then this program is for you! Fairies are magical, mystical, and enchanting. Fairies are everything that a child's dreams are made of. The Crafty Creations for this program are simple but will add so much to the experience. The Friendly Fairy will make your children feel that they can fly. Imagination is key at this age, and by providing the appropriate tools we can help to foster lifelong learners.

Books to Share

Fairy Houses by Tracy L. Kane

The Paper Princess by Elisa Kleven

Stella, Fairy of the Forest by Marie-Louise Gay

The Wizard, the Fairy and the Magic Chicken by Helen Lester

Good Night Fairies by Kathleen Hague

The Sleep Fairy by Janie Peterson

Great Game

Little Rabbit Foo Foo

(Tune: Down by the Station)

Little Rabbit Foo Foo
Hoppin' through the forest,
Scoopin' up the field mice
And kissin' them on the head.

Down came the good fairy,
And she said, "Little Rabbit Foo Foo,
I don't want to see you
Scoopin' up the field mice
And kissin' them on the head.
I'll give you 2 more chances . . .

And if you don't listen
I'll TURN YOU INTO A LOON!"

(Repeat until the rabbit uses its last chance and then the Good Fairy says . . .)

"Little Rabbit Foo Foo
I didn't want to see you
Scoopin' up the field mice
And kissin' them on the head.
I gave you 3 chances . . . and now . . .
POOF! You're a LOON!"

> ***Fun Factor***—After the children have learned this song you can add to it by bringing a crown, wand, and bunny ears to the circle. The children can take turns being the Good Fairy and Rabbit Foo Foo.

Fours and Fives: Fairy Folk

Rhymes and Songs

The Rainbow Fairies

(Photocopy seven of the Friendly Fairy Crafty Creation and colour them the colours mentioned in this rhyme.)

Two little clouds, one summer's day,
Went flying through the sky;
They went so fast they bumped their
heads,
And both began to cry. BOO-HOO!

Old Father Sun looked out and said:
"Oh, never mind, my dears,
I'll send my little fairy folk
To dry your falling tears."

One fairy came in violet,
And one wore indigo;
In blue, green, yellow, orange, red,
They made a pretty row.

They wiped the cloud-tears all away,
And then from out of the sky,
Upon a line the sunbeams made,
They hung their gowns to dry.

Fairy Ring

(Said quietly. This is a great quieting song for your group once you are all sitting together in a circle or on a carpeted area.)

If you see a fairy ring
In a field of grass,
Very lightly step around,
And tiptoe as you pass.
Last night fairies frolicked there,
And they're sleeping somewhere near.
Shhhhh . . .

If you see a tiny fairy
Lying fast asleep,
Shut your eyes,

(Close your eyes.)

And run away,

(Pretend to run.)

Do not stay to peep;

(Peek through your fingers.)

And be sure you never tell,
Or you'll break the fairy spell.

(Shake your head no.)

Fairy Dance

(Tune: Mulberry Bush)
(Suit actions to words.)
(Have children form a circle and all join hands to dance together.)

This is the way the fairies dance,
Fairies dance, fairies dance.
This is the way the fairies dance,
All night long.

Additional verses:

This is the way the fairies skip, run, jump,
clap . . .

Fairies in the Yard

(Tune: Wheels on the Bus)
(Suit actions to words.)

Fairies in the yard are flying around,
Flying around, flying around.
Fairies in the yard are flying around,
All around the yard.

Additional verses:

Twirling, skipping, hopping . . .

From Beth Maddigan and Stefanie Drennan, *The BIG Book of Reading, Rhyming, and Resources: Programs for Children Ages 4-8*. Westport, CT: Libraries Unlimited. © 2005.

Fours and Fives: Fairy Folk

Punchinello

(This is a great game to play with your group. Have children sit in a circle and choose one child to begin the game.)

Look who is here Punchinello funny
    fellow,
Look who is here Punchinello funny you.

What can you do Punchinello funny
    fellow?
What can you do Punchinello funny you?

(Have the child perform any action such as hand clapping, foot stomping . . .)

We can do it too Punchinello funny
    fellow.
We can do it too Punchinello funny you.

(Have the group repeat the action.)

(Continue until all of the children have had a turn to be Punchinello.)

10 Little Butterflies

(Tune: 10 Little Witches)
(Use your fingers to represent the butterflies in this song.)

1 little, 2 little, 3 little butterflies,
4 little, 5 little, 6 little butterflies,
7 little, 8 little, 9 little butterflies,
10 little butterfly friends.

They flutter and they flutter and they
    flutter all together,

(Wiggle your fingers in a fluttering motion.)

Flutter and they flutter and they flutter all
    together,
Flutter and they flutter and they flutter all
    together,
10 little butterfly friends.

Butterfly, Butterfly

(Hook your thumbs together and pretend your hands are butterfly wings.)

Butterfly, butterfly with wings light and
    airy,
Dance through the air like a tiny fairy.
Dance on the flower tops,
Dance on the trees.
Dance on the window ledge,
And dance on me!

Little Shadow

(Do the actions indicated.)

There is a little shadow
That dances on my wall.
Sometimes it's big and scary,

(Stand up very tall.)

Sometimes it's very small.

(Crouch down low.)

Sometimes it's oh so quiet,

(Place a finger on your lips.)

And doesn't move at all.

(Stand very still.)

Then other times it chases me,

(Run on the spot.)

Or bounces like a ball.

(Jump up and down.)

I'd love to meet that shadow,
Who dances in the night.
But it always runs away,
When I turn on my light!

Fours and Fives: Fairy Folk

Crafty Creation

Friendly Fairy

Materials

1 long craft or bamboo stick

1 photocopied fairy

Cardstock or poster board

Tissue paper—various colours

Glue

Tape

Scissors

Decorating materials—glitter, crayons, markers, feathers

Instructions

1. Photocopy the fairy template (enlarging it to the desired size) and glue it onto cardstock or poster board to make it sturdier.

2. Cut the tissue paper into thin strips (.4 inch wide by 4 inches long/1 cm wide by 10 cm long).

3. Cut out the fairy and tape the bamboo or craft stick onto the back.

4. Let the children colour or decorate their fairy friend.

From Beth Maddigan and Stefanie Drennan, *The BIG Book of Reading, Rhyming, and Resources: Programs for Children Ages 4-8*. Westport, CT: Libraries Unlimited. © 2005.

Fours and Fives: Fairy Folk

Fours and Fives: Fairy Folk

Crafty Creation

Creative Crown

Handy Hint*—Save time by cutting pieces of masking tape* about 3 inches/8 cm long ahead of time and taping them on a wall near your craft area.

Materials

White poster board or poster paper

Tissue paper—various colours

Glue sticks

Pipe cleaners—2 per child

Construction paper—various colours

Masking tape

Decorating materials—glitter, markers, stickers

Instructions

1. Fold the poster board sheet in half (left to right) end to end and then end to end again. Cut along the folded lines; you should have four strips of poster board long enough to fit around a child's head. This is the crown that the children will decorate.

2. Photocopy the butterfly template (to whatever size you like) and trace it onto various colours of construction paper. Cut the butterflies out and set them aside.

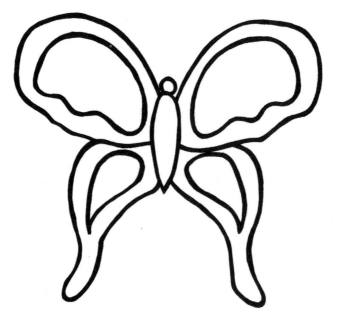

From Beth Maddigan and Stefanie Drennan, *The BIG Book of Reading, Rhyming, and Resources: Programs for Children Ages 4-8*. Westport, CT: Libraries Unlimited. © 2005.

60

Fours and Fives: Fairy Folk

3. Wrap the pipe cleaners around a pencil to make a "spring." Straighten about ½ inch/1.5 cm at the top and bottom of the spring (so it's easier tape on the butterflies).

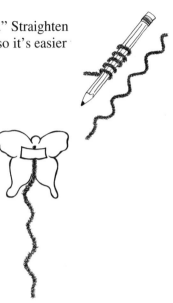

4. Tape a butterfly onto the top of each pipe cleaner.

5. Tape both pipe cleaners to the long piece of construction paper so they sit either at the front of the head or the side of the head.

6. Let the children decorate the crown with tissue paper or other decorating materials.

7. Tape the poster board ends together to form a crown and put it on.

From Beth Maddigan and Stefanie Drennan, *The BIG Book of Reading, Rhyming, and Resources: Programs for Children Ages 4-8*. Westport, CT: Libraries Unlimited. © 2005.

Fours and Fives: Forest Friends

This is a great way to expand on your animal themes. Talking about the animals of the forest instead of zoo or farm animals offers something a little different for your group to learn about. The Be-Whoo-Tiful Owl Crafty Creation is a great extension of the songs and stories listed in this program and is super easy to complete.

Books to Share

Little Bunny Foo Foo: A Cautionary Tale by the Good Fairy by Paul Brett Johnson (Illustrator)

Skunks! by David T. Greenburg

The Gruffalo by Julia Donaldson

Bear Snores On by Karma Wilson

Bear Wants More by Karma Wilson

The Bear Came Over to My House by Rick Walton

Great Game

Bunny, Bunny, Skunk

A new twist on an old and familiar favourite. Sit your group in a circle and pick someone to begin the game. The child who begins the game will walk slowly around the circle tapping each child that he or she passes lightly on the head. As each head is tapped, the child will say "Bunny" or "Skunk." If the child who is leading the game says skunk, the child who was named skunk must get up and move quickly around the circle, trying to beat the leader back to his or her spot in the circle.

The game ends when each child has had a turn to be either the leader or the skunk.

Fours and Fives: Forest Friends

Old Roger

(Tune: The Mulberry Bush)
(Have the children sit in a circle. Choose one child to be Old Roger, one child to be an apple tree, and one child to be the Old Lady. Start with Old Roger sleeping in the middle of the circle.)

> Old Roger was sleeping so sound in the
>   grass,
> Sound in the grass, sound in the grass.
> Old Roger was sleeping so sound in the
>   grass,
> Oh me, oh my, oh me.

(Have the child who is the apple tree stand over Old Roger with one foot on either side of his or her body.)

> They planted an apple tree over his head,
> Over his head, over his head.
> They planted an apple tree over his head,
> Oh me, oh my, oh me.

(Flutter your fingers downward to represent the apples falling.)

> The apples got ripe and they all fell down,
> All fell down, all fell down.
> The apples got ripe and they all fell down,
> Oh me, oh my, oh me.

(Have the child who is the Old Lady pretend to be picking apples off the floor.)

> There came an old lady a-picking them up,
> Picking them up, picking them up.
> There came an old lady a-picking them up,
> Oh me, oh my, oh me.

(Sing this verse quickly while clapping your hands. Old Roger should wake up and "chase" the Old Lady back to her spot in the circle.)

> Old Roger woke up and he chased her
>   away,
> Chased her away, chased her away.
> Old Roger woke up and he chased her
>   away,
> Oh me, oh my, oh me!

The Green Grass Grows

(This is a progressive song using repetition. Explain to the children that they should repeat after you, and after the first few verses they may start to sing along.)

> There was a tree *(Repeat.)*
> All in the wood *(Repeat.)*
> The prettiest tree *(Repeat.)*
> That you ever did see. *(Repeat.)*
> The tree in the hole and the hole in the
>   ground,
> And the green grass grows all around, all
>   around.
> And the green grass grows all around.
>
> And on that tree *(Repeat.)*
> There was a limb *(Repeat.)*
> The prettiest limb *(Repeat.)*
> That you ever did see. *(Repeat.)*
> Well the limb on the tree and the tree in
>   the hole,
> And the hole in the ground,
> And the green grass grows all around, all
>   around,
> And the green grass grows all around.

Additional verses:

> On that limb . . . there was a branch
> On that branch . . . there was a nest
> In that nest . . . there was an egg
> In that egg . . . there was a bird
> On that bird . . . there was a feather

From Beth Maddigan and Stefanie Drennan, *The BIG Book of Reading, Rhyming, and Resources: Programs for Children Ages 4-8*. Westport, CT: Libraries Unlimited. © 2005.

Fours and Fives: Forest Friends

Wide Eyed Owl

(Suit actions to words.)

There's a wide-eyed owl
With a pointed nose,
With two pointed ears
And claws for his toes.
He lives high in a tree
And when he looks down at you,
He flaps his wings
And he says, "Whoo, whoo."

5 Saucy Owls

(Use your fingers to represent the owls.)

Down on the corner in a great big tree,
There were 5 saucy owls just staring at me.
Along came kitty cat quiet as can be,
And she scared 1 owl right out of that tree!

4, 3, 2, 1

Brown Squirrel

Brown squirrel, brown squirrel
Shake your bushy tail.

(Wiggle your hips.)

Brown squirrel, brown squirrel,
Shake your bushy tail.

(Wiggle your hips.)

Wrinkle up your little nose,

(Wrinkle your nose.)

Put a nut between your toes,

(Pretend to hold a nut.)

Brown squirrel, brown squirrel,
Shake your bushy tail!

(Wiggle your hips.)

The Bat

This is my friend the bat,
He moves his wings this way and that.

(Sway from side to side.)

He swoops down low to eat his dinner,
(Bend down low.)
Then he flies up high where the air is
thinner.
(Stand up and pretend to fly.)
He sleeps in the day and he plays all night,
But you can hardly ever see him—he's
always out of sight.
(Hide your eyes.)

The Squirrel

(Suit actions to words.)

Whisky, frisky,
Hippity, hop!
Up he goes
To the tall tree top!

Whirly, twirly,
Round and round.
Down he scampers
To the ground.

Furly, curly,
What a tail!
Tall as a feather,
And broad as a sail!

Where's his supper?
In a shell,
Snappity, crackity,
Out it fell!

Little Squirrel

(Suit actions to words.)

This is the tall tree bare and brown,
And these are the fall leaves fluttering
down.
This is the little squirrel with eyes so
bright,
Hunting for nuts with all her might.
This is the hole where day by day,
Nut after nut she stores away.
When winter comes with its cold and storm,
She'll sleep all curled up all snug and warm.

From Beth Maddigan and Stefanie Drennan, *The BIG Book of Reading, Rhyming, and Resources: Programs for Children Ages 4-8*. Westport, CT: Libraries Unlimited. © 2005.

Fours and Fives: Forest Friends

Crafty Creation

Be-Whoo-Tiful Owl

Materials

Construction paper—brown, white, orange, and yellow

Scissors

Glue sticks

Decorating materials—markers, crayons, feathers

Instructions

1. Photocopy (and enlarge) or draw freehand the heart templates and cut out all pieces. Back them onto poster board or cardstock to make them sturdier, as these will be your tracers.

2. Cut out one large heart from brown construction paper, one medium heart from white paper, one small heart from orange paper, and two more small hearts from yellow paper.

3. Glue the medium-sized heart onto the largest heart so the tips touch.

4. Glue the orange small heart onto the owl just below the eyes to form the beak.

5. Glue the last two small hearts to the owl to form the feet.

6. Let the children decorate the owl using various decorating materials.

From Beth Maddigan and Stefanie Drennan, *The BIG Book of Reading, Rhyming, and Resources: Programs for Children Ages 4-8*. Westport, CT: Libraries Unlimited. © 2005.

Fours and Fives: Forest Friends

From Beth Maddigan and Stefanie Drennan, *The BIG Book of Reading, Rhyming, and Resources: Programs for Children Ages 4-8*. Westport, CT: Libraries Unlimited. © 2005.

Fours and Fives: Forest Friends

Breezy Bunny

This bunny is cute and a breeze to make!

Materials

White poster board (4 strips per sheet)—enough for your group

Tissue paper strips—various colours

String or yarn

Masking tape

Hole punch

Glue sticks

Decorating materials—markers, crayons, glitter

Instructions

1. Cut a sheet of poster board into four long strips.

2. Photocopy (and enlarge) the ear templates, back them with cardstock or poster board, and cut them out.

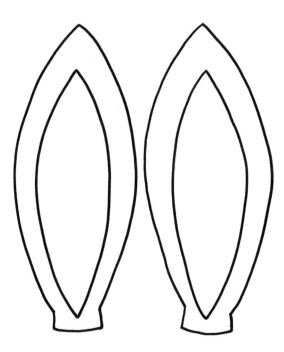

Fours and Fives: Forest Friends

3. Photocopy and then trace a set of ears for each child in your group (or draw them freehand) and cut them out.

4. Cut tissue paper into streamers 24 inches/60 cm long.

5. Cut yarn into pieces 12 inches/30 cm long (one per bunny)

6. Attach the ears towards the middle of the poster board strip. Check the positioning by holding the ends together to form the bunny's head (but don't secure the ends yet). Once you are satisfied with where the ears are, glue them into place.

7. Have the children draw the bunny's face, colour its ears, and, using a glue stick, attach streamers to the inside of the bunny's head. (To do this, they will need to put the bunny face down on the table in front of them.)

8. Once the decorating is complete, join the ends of the poster board to form a cylinder and secure them in place using masking tape.

9. Punch a hole on the left and right sides of the bunny (near the top) and tie the yarn on to form both the handle to carry it and the string to hang it with.

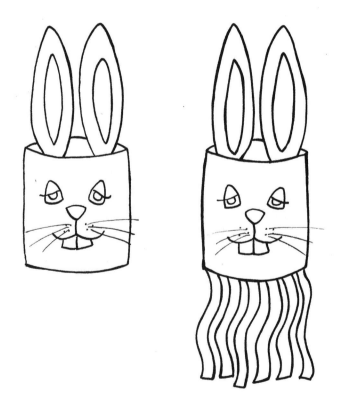

From Beth Maddigan and Stefanie Drennan, *The BIG Book of Reading, Rhyming, and Resources: Programs for Children Ages 4-8*. Westport, CT: Libraries Unlimited. © 2005.

Fours and Fives: Frosty Frolics

Take a walk in a winter wonderland. Once the weather turns colder, children's thoughts turn to slush . . . and ice and snow. With the snow comes snowsuits, hats, and of course mittens! The *Who's Got a Mitten* game is a great addition to this program because it gets everyone involved and helps the children with pattern recognition. Be sure to make enough mittens for everyone.

Books to Share

The Mitten by Alvin Tresselt

Jillian Jiggs and the Great Big Snow by Phoebe Gilman

Tacky the Penguin by Helen Lester

There Was a Cold Lady Who Swallowed Some Snow by Lucille Colandro

The Emperor's Egg by Martin Jenkins

Snow Music by Lynne Rae Perkins

Great Game

Who's Got a Mitten?

Getting started: Bring in a laundry basket from home to use with this game. You will need one unique pair of mittens for every child in your group. The mittens can be real (if you know a knitter or have a secondhand clothing store nearby), or you can create them using the mitten templates in the next activity. If you are making the mittens, design each pair with a distinctive pattern.

When you are ready to play: Sort the mittens by separating each pair into two piles. Give the children in your group one mitten each from one pile and keep the other pile next to you. Choose a mitten from the pile and say:

Who has a mitten like this one?
Who has a mitten like me?
Who has a mitten like this one?
Stand up and let me see.

The child with the matching mitten will stand up. Call the child to the front and give him or her your mitten. He or she should then put the pair in the designated spot.

Fun Factor—Using yarn and masking tape, string up a "clothesline" near your program area for the children to hang the mittens on when they have their pair. Bring in clothespins from home or visit your local discount store to purchase pins made of colourful plastic.

From Beth Maddigan and Stefanie Drennan, *The BIG Book of Reading, Rhyming, and Resources: Programs for Children Ages 4-8*. Westport, CT: Libraries Unlimited. © 2005.

Fours and Fives: Frosty Frolics

Rhymes and Songs

Once There Was a Snowman

(Have your group stand and pretend to be the snowman.)

> Once there was a snowman, snowman,
>   snowman,
> Once there was a snowman, tall, tall, tall.

(Stand up very tall.)

> And in the sun he melted, melted, melted,
> And in the sun he melted, small, small, small.

(Pretend to melt and crouch down to the floor.)

The Snowman Pokey

(Tune: The Hokey Pokey)

> You put your right mitten in,
> You take your right mitten out.
> You put your right mitten in,
> And you shake it all about.
> You do the snowman pokey,
> And you turn yourself around,
> That's what it's all about!

Additional Verses:

> Put your left mitten in . . .
> Put your long scarf in . . .
> Put your top hat in . . .
> Put your carrot nose in . . .
> Put your snowself in . . .

6 Little Penguins

(Tune: 6 Little Ducks)

> 6 little penguins I once knew,
> Short and stout, fancy dressed ones too.
> But the first little penguin walking side to
>   side,
> He led the others with a slip, slip, slide.

> Slip, slip, slide.
> Slip, slip, slide.
> He led the others with a slip, slip, slide.

> Down to the water they would dash,
> Waddle, waddle, waddle, waddle.
> Splash! Splash! Splash!
> But the first little penguin walking side to
>   side,
> He led the others with a slip, slip, slide.
> Slip, slip, slide.
> Slip, slip, slide.
> He led the others with a slip, slip, slide.

> Up from the water they would stroll,
> The penguins go parading out in the cold.
> But the one little penguin walking side to
>   side,
> He led the others with a slip, slip, slide.
> Slip, slip, slide.
> Slip, slip, slide.
> He led the others with a slip, slip, slide.

Have You Ever Seen a Penguin?

(Tune: Have You Ever Seen a Lassie?)

> Have you ever seen a penguin, a penguin,
>   a penguin,
> Have you ever seen a penguin swim this
>   way and that?
> Swim this way and that way,
> And this way and that way.
> Have you ever seen a penguin swim this
>   way and that?

Additional verses:

> Have you ever seen a penguin slide this
>   way and that?
> Have you ever seen a penguin waddle this
>   way and that?

From Beth Maddigan and Stefanie Drennan, *The BIG Book of Reading, Rhyming, and Resources: Programs for Children Ages 4-8.* Westport, CT: Libraries Unlimited. © 2005.

Fours and Fives: Frosty Frolics

10 Little Penguins

(Tune: 10 Little Witches)

1 little, 2 little, 3 little penguins,
4 little, 5 little, 6 little penguins,
7 little, 8 little, 9 little penguins,
10 little penguin chicks.

They waddle and they waddle and they
    waddle all together,
Waddle and they waddle and they waddle
    all together,
Waddle and they waddle and they waddle
    all together,
10 little penguin chicks.

(Repeat first verse.)

They slip and they slide and they play all
    together,
Slip and they slide and they play all
    together,
Slip and they slide and they play all
    together,
10 little penguin chicks.

I'm a Little Penguin

(Tune: I'm a Little Teapot)

I'm a little penguin black and white,
Short and wobbly, an adorable sight.
I can't fly at all but I love to swim,
So I waddle to the water and I dive right in.

I'm a little penguin on the ice,
I think the cold is very nice.
I can hop around first once then twice,
I think ice is very nice.

Mittens

Mittens for the winter,
When the world is white.
Mittens for my left hand,

(Hold up left hand.)

Mittens for my right.

(Hold up right hand.)

Mittens with a thumb place,

(Hold up thumbs.)

Mittens warm and snug.

(Hug yourself.)

Mittens warm my hands like a bug in rug!

The Mitten in the Snow

(Tune: The Farmer in the Dell)
(This song goes with the Alvin Tresselt book The Mitten. In the second verse, fill in the blank with the animals in the order that they appear in the book and crawl into the mitten.)

The mitten in the snow,
The mitten in the snow,
Help us please so we won't freeze!
The mitten in the snow.

The _____ squeezes in,
The _____ squeezes in,
Help us please so we won't freeze!
The _____ squeezes in.

(Make an extra copy of the Mitten Magic craft and use it to accompany this song, or make enough extra copies of the animals to distribute to your group. When you sing about a particular animal, all of the children with that animal can come to the front and put their animal in the mitten.)

From Beth Maddigan and Stefanie Drennan, *The BIG Book of Reading, Rhyming, and Resources: Programs for Children Ages 4-8*. Westport, CT: Libraries Unlimited. © 2005.

Fours and Fives: Frosty Frolics

Crafty Creation

Mitten Magic

A great accompanying craft to Alvin Tresselt's must-read story!

Materials

Paper lunch bags, enough for your group

Glue sticks

Popsicle sticks

Masking tape

Photocopy paper—assorted colours

Decorating materials—crayons, markers, cotton balls, bingo dabbers

Instructions

1. Photocopy (and enlarge) the mitten templates onto various colours of photocopy paper (or leave them white and let the children colour them) and cut them out.

2. Glue one mitten on one side of the paper bag and its mate on the other side.

3. Photocopy or cut out animal pictures from old newspapers, magazines, clip-art books, etc., and let the children choose their own animals to use with their mittens.

4. Using masking tape, tape the Popsicle sticks to the back of the animals.

5. The children can use the animals to tell their own stories and then put them into the bags to take them home.

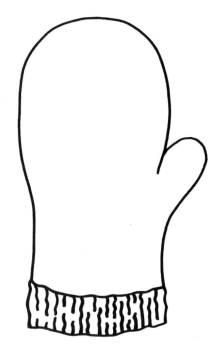

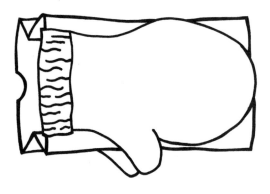

From Beth Maddigan and Stefanie Drennan, *The BIG Book of Reading, Rhyming, and Resources: Programs for Children Ages 4-8*. Westport, CT: Libraries Unlimited. © 2005.

Fours and Fives : Frosty Frolics

Crafty Creation

Portly Penguin

Fun and easy to make, this craft takes no time at all to create and decorate!

Materials

2 Styrofoam cups per child

Black construction paper

Yellow construction paper

White paper

Scissors

Masking tape

Decorating materials—crayons, cotton balls

Glue sticks

Instructions

1. Take your Styrofoam cups and put one on top of the other so the tops are facing, then tape them together (this will be your penguin's body).

2. Photocopy (and enlarge) and cut out the templates of the wings, beak, and feet. Back them onto sturdy paper so that they can serve as tracers.

From Beth Maddigan and Stefanie Drennan, *The BIG Book of Reading, Rhyming, and Resources: Programs for Children Ages 4-8*. Westport, CT: Libraries Unlimited. © 2005.

Fours and Fives: Frosty Frolics

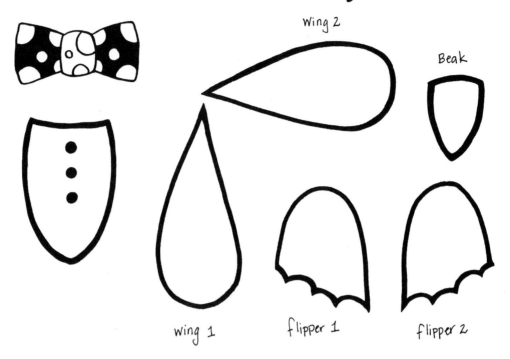

3. Using a pencil, trace the wings onto black construction paper and cut them out.

4. Tape the wings onto the sides of the penguin's body.

5. Next, trace the beak and feet onto yellow construction paper and cut them out.

6. Tape or glue the feet to the bottom of the cup so that they stick out and glue the penguin's mouth onto the front of the cup. (See illustration of the final craft.)

7. Cut out eyes from black construction paper (sized to the penguin) and put a little white circle (sized to the black circle) in the middle. Glue on.

8. Let the children decorate with cotton balls to add fur or colour with crayons.

From Beth Maddigan and Stefanie Drennan, *The BIG Book of Reading, Rhyming, and Resources: Programs for Children Ages 4-8*. Westport, CT: Libraries Unlimited. © 2005.

Fours and Fives: Just for Fun

The final program in this chapter is well suited to its name: Just for fun. This program is great for when you feel that you have covered every topic you think imaginable or . . . just for fun! The songs are full of action to get your group up and moving and are great to use not only with this program but also as a back-pocket tool to keep on hand in case you find your group getting restless in any program. They really are a lot of fun and are sure to become group favourites in no time.

Books to Share

King Bidgood's in the Bathtub by Audrey Wood

Jamberry by Bruce Degen

Big Bear Ball by Joanne Ryder

How Can You Dance? by Rick Walton

Giraffes Can't Dance by Giles Andreae

Down by the Cool of the Pool by Tony Mitton

Great Game

Monkey See, Monkey Do

Everyone forms a circle; one participant (the monkey) goes to the middle and makes up a dance or movement for everyone else to imitate, then takes a bow and moves to the outside. All participants get a chance to be the monkey separately. At the end of the song everyone steps in the middle to do all the new movements initiated by all the monkeys.

Monkey see, monkey do.
Do you want to be a monkey, too?
(Choose a child to be the monkey in the middle.)
There's a monkey in the middle, just because,
You've got to do what that little monkey does.
(The "monkey" performs an action and everyone else follows along.)
Chorus:
Now the monkey in the middle takes a bow,
(Child takes a bow and rejoins the circle.)
There's a new little monkey gonna show us how.
(Choose a new child to be the monkey.)
Monkey's in the middle, just because,
You've got to do what that little monkey does.
(Continue until everyone has had a turn to be the monkey, and end with the following verse:)
Monkey see, monkey do.
Step in the middle, be a monkey too.
(Step into the middle and do all of the different actions.)
We're all monkeys in the middle, just because
We can do anything any monkey does.

From Beth Maddigan and Stefanie Drennan, *The BIG Book of Reading, Rhyming, and Resources: Programs for Children Ages 4-8*. Westport, CT: Libraries Unlimited. © 2005.

Fours and Fives: Just for Fun

Rhymes and Songs

One Finger

(Tune: The Bear Went Over the Mountain)
(A progressive song that will get everyone involved.)

One finger, one thumb, keep moving,

(Tap your thumb and index finger as you sing.)

One finger, one thumb, keep moving,
One finger, one thumb, keep moving,
We'll all be merry and bright.

Additional verses:

One finger, one thumb, one arm, keep
moving
One finger, one thumb, one arm, one leg,
keep moving
One finger, one thumb, one arm, one leg,
one nod of the head, keep moving
One finger, one thumb, one arm, one leg,
one nod of the head, stand up-sit down,
keep moving

My Bubble Flew Over the Ocean

(Tune: My Bonnie Lies Over the Ocean)
(Stand up and sit down every time a word beginning with b is sung.)

My bubble flew over the ocean,
(Stand up.)
My bubble flew over the sea.
(Sit down.)
My bubble flew over the ocean,
(Stand up.)
Oh, bring back my bubble to me.
(Sit, stand, Sit.)
Bring back, bring back,
(Stand then sit, stand then sit.)
Oh, bring back my bubble to me, to me.

(Stand, sit, stand.)
Bring back, bring back,
(Sit then stand, sit then stand.)
Oh, bring back my bubble to me.
(Sit, stand, sit.)

Johnny Works with One Hammer

(This song can be sung with your group sitting or standing.)

Johnny works with one hammer, one
hammer, one hammer.
Johnny works with one hammer.
(Pound air with fist.)
Now he works with two.
(Start with other hand.)
Additional verses:

Johnny works with two hammers . . .
Johnny works with three hammers . . .
(Stamp foot.)
Johnny works with four hammers . . .
(Alternate stamping feet.)
Johnny works with five hammers . . .
(Now he goes to sleep. Nod head.)

Clap, Jump, Hop

(Tune: Skip to My Lou)
(Suit actions to words.)

Clap, clap, clap and turn around,
Jump, jump, jump and touch the ground.
Hop, hop, hop and touch your nose,
Clap again and touch your toes.

Clap, clap, clap, and turn around,
Tap, tap, tap and touch the ground.
Snap, snap, snap your fingers loud,
Clap again and then sit down.

From Beth Maddigan and Stefanie Drennan, *The BIG Book of Reading, Rhyming, and Resources: Programs for Children Ages 4-8.* Westport, CT: Libraries Unlimited. © 2005.

Fours and Fives: Just for Fun

When I Was a Sailor

(Gather your group into a circle to begin this action rhyme. After reciting the poem, point to a child in the circle to perform the action to finish the rhyme; for example, for the line "When I was a driver, this is what I did" the child could pretend to be driving a car. Choose a new child when you choose a new job.)

When I was a sailor, a sailor, a sailor,
When I was a sailor, this is what I did.

Additional verses

When I was a driver, this is what I did.
When I was a tailor, this is what I did.
When I was a doctor, this is what I did.
When I was a carpenter, this is what I did.

My Name Is Joe

(Suit actions to words.)
(A familiar favourite full of action!)

Hello my name is Joe and I work in a
    button factory
I have a house, and a dog, and a family
One day, my boss said to me, "Hey Joe,
    are you busy?"
I said, "No."
He said "Push the button with your left
    hand."

(Pretend to push a button continuously with your left hand.)

Hello my name is Joe and I work in a
    button factory
I have a house, and a dog, and a family
One day, my boss said to me, "Hey Joe,
    are you busy?"
I said, "No."
He said "Push the button with your right
    hand."

(Pretend to push two buttons as you sing.)

Hello my name is Joe and I work in a
    button factory
I have a house, and a dog, and a family
One day, my boss said to me, "Hey Joe,
    are you busy?"
I said, "No."
He said "Push the button with your left
    foot."

(Pretend to push buttons with both hands and one foot as you sing.)

Hello my name is Joe and I work in a
    button factory
I have a house, and a dog, and a family
One day, my boss said to me, "Hey Joe,
    are you busy?"
I said, "No."
He said "Push the button with your right
    foot."

(Pretend to push buttons with both hands and both feet as you sing.)

Hello my name is Joe and I work (real
    hard) in a button factory
I have a house, and a dog, and a family
One day, my boss said to me, "Hey Joe,
    are you busy?"
I said, "No."
He said "Push the button with your head."

(Pretend to push buttons with your hands, feet, and head as you sing.)

Hello my name is Joe and I work in a
    button factory
I have a house, and a dog, and a family
One day, my boss said to me, "Hey Joe,
    are you busy?"
I said, "Yes!!!"

(Collapse in a heap on the floor or in a chair.)

From Beth Maddigan and Stefanie Drennan, *The BIG Book of Reading, Rhyming, and Resources: Programs for Children Ages 4-8.* Westport, CT: Libraries Unlimited. © 2005.

Fours and Fives: Just for Fun

Clap, Two, Three, Four!

(Suit actions to words.)

Clap, two, three, four, five, six, seven.

(Clap hands.)

Shake, two, three, four, five, six, seven.

(Shake fingers.)

Slap, two, three, four, five, six, seven.

(Slap table or knees. Not too hard!)

Roll, two, three, four, five, six, seven.

(Rotate one hand around the other.)

Snap, two, three, four, five, six, seven.

(Snap fingers.)

Tap, two, three, four, five, six, seven.

(Pound fists.)

Push, two, three, four, five, six, seven.

(Push hands forward.)

Clap, two, three, four, five, six, seven.

(Clap hands.)

Now, shake your hands and clap, clap,
  clap
Shake your hands and fold them in your
  lap.

As I Was Walking

(For this song, you will need an old broom-stick handle or yard ruler to be the fallen tree. Start by having your group stand in a circle. The programmer can either sit or stand as he or she sings. Hold the broomstick over your head as you sing the first two lines. When you sing the line "I . . . heard a crack, the tree fell down," bring the broomstick down to the floor and have the children go over, under, or around it. You can also let the children make up different ways to get home.)

As I was walking homeward bound,
One dark and storm-y night.
I . . . heard a crack,
A tree fell down,
And I went home—going my way.

And I went . . . over . . . over
I made it home by going over the tree.
And I went . . . over . . . over,
I made it home by going over the tree

Additional verses:

Under *(Lift the broomstick up so that
  children can go under it.)*
Around it *(Put the broomstick flat on the
  ground and have children walk around it.)*

From Beth Maddigan and Stefanie Drennan, *The BIG Book of Reading, Rhyming, and Resources: Programs for Children Ages 4-8*. Westport, CT: Libraries Unlimited. © 2005.

Fours and Fives: Just for Fun

Crafty Creation

Super Sailboats

More than just a craft, these sailboats really float!

Materials

Plastic lids (from margarine tubs)—enough for your group

Drinking straws—enough for your group

Construction paper—various colours

Scissors

Hole punch

Play dough—enough for a piece the size of a ping pong ball for each child (see recipe in next activity)

Decorating materials—crayons, markers, stickers, bingo dabbers

Instructions

1. Photocopy (and enlarge) the triangle template and cut it out. (Back it with poster board or cardstock to make it sturdier, as this will be your tracer.)

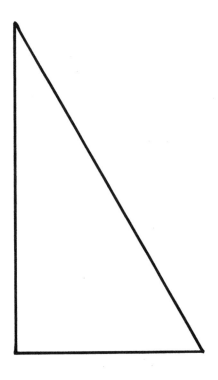

Fours and Fives: Just for Fun

2. Trace the triangle onto different colours of construction paper and cut out enough sails for your group.

3. Punch three holes along the long side of the triangle and weave a drinking straw (the boat's mast) through the holes.

4. Let the children decorate their boat's mast before doing the next step.

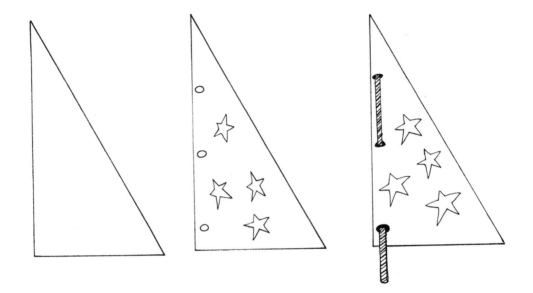

5. Put the small piece of play dough on the inside of the lid and push the drinking straw into it.

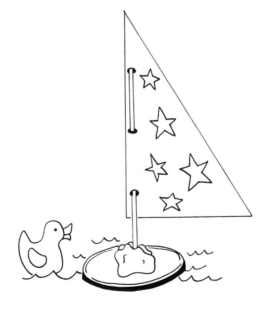

Fours and Fives: Just for Fun

Crafty Creation

Play Dough Recipe

Instead of buying commercial play dough for your group to use, why not make your own? It's really not that hard, and you can be creative by mixing your own colours.

Materials

1 cup flour

1 cup warm water

2 teaspoons cream of tartar

1 teaspoon oil

¼ cup salt

Food colouring (any colours)

Instructions

1. Mix all ingredients, adding food colouring last, in a medium pot.

2. Stir over medium heat until smooth.

3. Remove from pot and knead, on a lightly floured surface, until blended and smooth.

4. When it is cooled, place it in a plastic bag or airtight container. It will last for a couple of weeks.

> *Fun Factor*—To make the experience a little more sensory, mix a small package of unsweetened drink mix powder (grape, cherry) to the warm water instead of using food colouring. Not only will your boats float, the colours will be vibrant and they will smell great!

From Beth Maddigan and Stefanie Drennan, *The BIG Book of Reading, Rhyming, and Resources: Programs for Children Ages 4-8*. Westport, CT: Libraries Unlimited. © 2005.

Fours and Fives: Just for Fun

Crafty Creation

Piece-of-Cake Puzzle

Materials

Craft sticks/tongue depressors—7 per child

Markers or crayons

Masking tape

Black permanent marker

Instructions

1.   Photocopy (and enlarge) and cut out the template of your choice. Back it onto sturdy paper, as this will be your tracer.

From Beth Maddigan and Stefanie Drennan, *The BIG Book of Reading, Rhyming, and Resources: Programs for Children Ages 4-8*. Westport, CT: Libraries Unlimited. © 2005.

82

Fours and Fives: Just for Fun

2. Line the tongue depressors up horizontally in front of you (see illustration).

3. Tape two long strips of masking tape, vertically, on the left and right sides of the puzzle and trim off the excess at the ends.

4. Using a black marker, start at the top tongue depressor and put the numbers from 1 to 7 (working down) on each tongue depressor. This will help to put the puzzle in order in case anyone needs help.

5. Flip the puzzle over and choose a tracer. Using a black marker, trace around the tracer, leaving a black outline to colour inside.

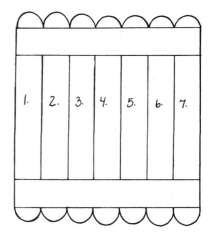

6. Have the children colour in their puzzles however they choose.

7. Separate the sticks to make the puzzle pieces.

If you don't have tongue depressor-sized craft sticks, you can use 10 Popsicle sticks instead.

From Beth Maddigan and Stefanie Drennan, *The BIG Book of Reading, Rhyming, and Resources: Programs for Children Ages 4-8*. Westport, CT: Libraries Unlimited. © 2005.

Bibliography of Books to Share

Andreae, Giles. 2001. *Giraffes Can't Dance*. New York: Scholastic.

Barner, Bob. 1999. *Bugs! Bugs! Bugs!* San Francisco: Chronicle Books.

Brown, Ken. 2001. *The Scarecrow's Hat*. Atlanta, GA: Peachtree Publishers.

Colandro, Lucy. 2002. *There Was a Cold Lady Who Swallowed Some Snow*. New York: Cartwheel Books.

Cooper, Helen. 1999. *Pumpkin Soup*. New York: Farrar, Straus & Giroux.

Degen, Bruce. 1983. *Jamberry*. New York: HarperCollins.

Donaldson, Julia. 1999. *The Gruffalo*. New York: Dial Books.

Galloway, Ruth. 2003. *Fidgety Fish*. Alpharetta, GA: Tiger Tales.

Galloway, Ruth. 2002. *Smiley Shark*. Alpharetta, GA: Tiger Tales.

Gay, Marie Louise. 2002. *Stella, Fairy of the Forest*. Toronto: Groundwood Books.

Gay, Marie Louise. 2004. *Stella, Star of the Sea*. Toronto: Groundwood Books.

Gibbons, Gail. 2000. *The Pumpkin Book*. New York: Holiday House.

Gilman, Phoebe. 2002. *Jillian Jiggs and the Great Big Snow*. Markham, ON: Northwinds Press.

Greenburg, David T. 1997. *Bugs!* New York: Scholastic.

Greenburg, David T. 2002. *Skunks!* New York: Little, Brown.

Hague, Kathleen. 2002. *Good Night Fairies*. San Francisco: Seastar Books.

Jenkins, Martin. 1999. *The Emperor's Egg*. Cambridge, MA: Candlewick Press.

Johnson, Paul Brett. 2002. *Little Bunny Foo Foo: A Cautionary Tale as Told by the Good Fairy*. New York: Scholastic Press.

Kane, Tracy L. 2001. *Fairy Houses*. Lee, NH: Great White Dog Picture Company.

Kleven, Elisa.1994. *The Paper Princess*. New York: Dutton Books.

Lester, Helen. 1990. *Tacky the Penguin*. Boston: Houghton Mifflin.

Lester, Helen. 1988. *The Wizard, the Fairy and the Magic Chicken*. Boston: Houghton Mifflin/Walter Lorraine Books.

Lilligard, Dee. 1999. *The Big Bug Ball*. New York: Penguin.

Little, Jean, et al. 1994. *Once Upon a Golden Apple*. New York: Penguin.

Mitton, Tony. 2002. *Down by the Cool of the Pool*. New York: Orchard Books.

Munsch, Robert. 1985. *Mortimer*. Toronto: Annick Press.

Perkins, Lynne Rae. 2002. *Snow Music*. New York: Greenwillow.

Peterson, Janie. 2002. *The Sleep Fairy*. Omaha, NE: Behave'N Kids Press.

Pledger, Maurice. 2001. *In the Ocean.* San Diego: Silver Dolphin.

Pratt, Kristin Joy. 1994. *A Swim Through the Sea.* Nevada, CA: Dawn Publications.

Priceman, Marjorie. 1996. *How to Make an Apple Pie and See the World.* Cleveland, OH: Dragonfly Books.

Ryder, Joanne. 2002. *Big Bear Ball.* New York: HarperCollins.

Shield, Carol Diggery. 2002. *The Bugliest Bug.* Cambridge, MA: Candlewick Press.

Stone, Rosetta. 1975. *Because a Little Bug Went Kachoo*! New York: Random House Books for Young Readers.

Tresselt, Alvin. 1989. *The Mitten.* New York: HarperTrophy.

Walton, Rick. 2002. *The Bear Came Over to My House.* New York: Puffin Books.

Walton, Rick. 2001. *How Can You Dance*? New York: G. P. Putnam's Sons.

Ward, Jennifer. 2000. *Somewhere in the Ocean.* Flagstaff, AZ: Rising Moon Books.

White, Linda. 1997. *Too Many Pumpkins.* New York: Holiday House.

Wilson, Karma. 2002. *Bear Snores On.* New York: Margaret McElderry.

Wilson, Karma. 2003. *Bear Wants More.* New York: Margaret McElderry.

Wood, Audrey. 1982. *King Bidgood's in the Bathtub.* Swindon, Bridgemead: Child's Play International.

Wood, Audrey. 1985. *Quick as a Cricket.* San Diego: Harcourt Children's Books.

Chapter 4

Six to Eight Year Olds: Ready, Set, Readers

Independent reading is a challenge children face early in their in formal schooling. As parents, educators, and programmers, we have been preparing children for the moment when the world of reading is open to them as individuals. We sing and rhyme with babies, model behaviours with toddlers, and expose preschoolers to stories in a variety of formats. But for six to eight year olds the preparation is over. They will now leap into the wonderful world of independent reading. This transition is not predictable or necessarily smooth. Much like the physical hurdle of taking those first few steps, unravelling the mystery of the written word can be a path with bumps and scrapes. At the library, we can use programs in a way that will make this transition easier, less stressful, and much, much more fun!

Should your facility develop a program to help *teach* children how to read? The answer to that question lies in the goals and objectives of your institution. If your centre has a mandate that specifically includes education and literacy, then the answer is yes. Many libraries and schools have had great success with "reading buddy" programs. These programs pair a confident older reader, that is, a senior elementary or junior high school student, with an emerging reader. The buddies practice reading, listening comprehension, and word games. The child learning to read gets to practice in an environment that is comforting, with a figure less authoritative than a parent or teacher. Mistakes are expected and not necessarily corrected. The buddy offers help only if asked. The emerging reader is simply given a time to practice that is stress free. The older student is also quite familiar with academic hurdles and can be sympathetic and supportive. This type of program will be especially popular and beneficial if a significant segment of the population in your catchment area has learned English as a second language. It is much easier to teach children to read and speak in their native tongue, so the extra help of a reading buddy program is often greatly appreciated by those learning English.

Should your facility continue to offer literature-based "storytime-style" programs such as those in the previous chapter? Absolutely! Even more important in a library or extracurriculum centre is a literature-based program that focuses on fun. Here is why the development of this type of program is beneficial for the children who will attend:

- **Read-alouds**—Emerging readers and newly confident readers need to have books read aloud to them. Their development and comprehension are at different stages, and the books they can read to themselves are often not as entertaining as the books they enjoy hearing.

- **Fun and games**—Reading will be work for children at this age and stage of development, and when you struggle with something it is easy to forget that it can also be fun! Literature-based programs are fun.

- **Associated activities**—Activities other than reading that foster different aspects of development, that is, gross and fine motor skills and cognitive development, can be bolstered and enhanced in programs through activities such as crafts and games. Allowing children to associate these other activities with reading will help to keep a positive focus, even for those children who find independent reading a struggle.

- **Recreational focus**—Six to eight year olds concentrate on reading during their formal schooling. By focusing on recreation, literature-based programs allow a group of children at widely different levels of reading comprehension to interact in an environment that is relaxed and stress free.

It is easy to become focused on reading as a milestone activity for emerging and newly confident readers. Literacy belongs in the curriculum and in programs for libraries and after-school centres that have it as a goal. However, all extracurricular and public library programs should keep recreation, positive literature-based experiences, and group activities at the forefront of programming objectives. Chapters 4 and 5 concentrate on programs that enhance those goals.

1. What Can Six, Seven, and Eight Year Olds Do?: Child Development for Six to Eight Year Olds

The three years from six to nine seem like a huge developmental span. However, children in this age group can really benefit from interacting and working together. They have developmental commonalities that assist the group dynamic. In addition, at school and in other recreational activities they will be divided more strictly according to age. In the programs you provide, younger children will benefit from seeing others who have achieved milestones they are working towards. Older children will get a sense of accomplishment from the respect they receive. In addition, brain development for specific skills (and reading is certainly included in these) is achieved at very different rates.

EXPERT ADVICE

To get the maximum benefit from your program for 6 to 8 year olds, divide the children into pairs and threes for activities whenever appropriate. Pair younger children with older children instead of letting groups choose themselves. The children will benefit from the interaction and competitions will be more evenly matched.

Instead of age-specific milestones, as we have identified for the previous chapter, children in this age group have a change in focus. Imagination and fantasy recede as peer interaction and problem solving come to the fore. So, what are the focus points for six- to eight-year-old children? Young school-age children are unconsciously concentrating on

- peer interaction, especially same-sex relationships;

- the difference between right and wrong and a desire to achieve;

- mistakes and a sensitivity to criticism;

- group activities and organized games;

- collecting, building, and grouping things into sets; and

- exploration, curiosity, and creativity.

Most six-year-old children will have reached a state of physical and intellectual development that will allow them to enjoy activities in a group with older children. Such accomplishments include

- use of scissors to cut simple objects;

- writing letters of the alphabet, especially to copy or write their own names;

- copying shapes, objects, colours, styles, and patterns;

- tying laces and strings;

- catching balls and small objects and tossing to a target;

- acrobatics such as tumbling and jumping; and

- an understanding of basic rules and an ability to follow simple directions.

Understanding six to eight year olds' focus and abilities will help you to develop programs that encourage their growth, development, and sense of fun. You will keep literature and reading in a positive light during what could be a difficult transition to independent reading.

2. Six to Eight Year Old Programming Guidelines

2.1 Starting a Program for Six to Eight Year Olds

To develop a program for six to eight year olds you must first identify your goals and objectives for working with this age group. If you are concentrating on literacy, the program would be better suited to a more discrete age grouping. If you have chosen goals such as a positive library experience, assisting children to learn how the library works, group and social development, or activity and recreational literary experiences (i.e., dramatic play, puppetry, magic, etc.) this age grouping will work quite well. To be successful with this group your literature-based program should concentrate on reading comprehension, group dynamics, and fun!

Timing is especially important. Children are in school for a full day. Plan your program with enough time for children to get home from school and have a snack, or provide them with one in the program. Consider mealtimes, homework, and bedtimes when choosing your program's start time. Late afternoon is a good time. You may also consider a weekend, but keep in mind other recreational activities that may conflict with your program, such as sports and music.

Preregistration of children in the group will allow you to organize structured activities and games, which children at this age enjoy. Advance registration will also allow children to develop relationships with the other children who come every week. However, children in this age group are ready to interact with peers, even new children they meet for the first time, so a drop-in program will also work quite well. Your drop-in program, however, should include games and activities that focus on individuals or on groups of *any* number. Be very careful not to structure an activity or game that may leave single a child without a partner or group. Six, seven, and eight year olds have a strong desire to fit in and will be sensitive to being left out.

BRIGHT IDEA

Feed their minds and bodies! Six to eight year olds attending afterschool programs may need a snack if they are coming directly from school. Contact local businesses such as restaurants and supermarkets to have healthy snacks donated. Concentrate on non-perishable items avaiable in single servings to avoid sharing germs. If you are offering food in a program, be sure to clear the menu with all parents first. Some children have severe allergies, and grown-ups may not think to share this information with you if they don't know snacks will be offered.

If your facility does not already have a program for this age group, it is important to market to existing groups of children and provide descriptive program titles that emphasize fun. Six, seven, and eight year olds will only partake in activities that interest them. They are also gaining the ability to veto decisions made by their parents. Therefore, while your program might appeal to mother and father, if it doesn't appeal to son and daughter, you may experience low registration numbers, especially in the seven- and eight-year-old range. Your program should focus on appealing activities and themes that are broad enough to engage a wide group of children. Young school-age children will want to have their friends join and take part as well, so the best programs run for a few consecutive weeks and have a broad, appealing title.

2.2 Getting Ready

Some of the key concepts for program preparation were addressed in the previous chapter. You will need all of those elements and more for children at this age. In addition to comfortable seating and a creative activity space, the room or area should be defined, safe, and clutter free. Six to eight year olds are very focused on their environment, and it is important to remove any program elements that would be identified with younger children. While it is fine to display art and activities from the "little kids" on the wall, it is imperative that blocks, toys, and games be kept out of sight, so children won't form an immediate impression that the program is too "baby-ish." Your space should be set up and ready when the children arrive. Six, seven, and eight year olds are critical and need to be entertained, or they will develop their own patterns of play and your suggestions and direction will be dismissed. Structure your program and develop an outline for each week. Have the elements ready beforehand so you can move from one activity to the next with minimal interruption. Structure and focus are very important for this age group. To keep the program's tone positive and upbeat, you will need to keep the flow and transitions moving smoothly. Happily, these children have much longer attention spans than do younger children, so you can develop activities and games that are more involved, that have rules, and that require direction.

What tools will you need for children at this age group? Discard the storytime apron and imaginative play toys. Focus on elements that will allow interaction or creative individual expression, such as

- an erasable wipe board and magnet board;

- a CD player with a selection of preteen and dance-able music;

- arts and crafts supplies;

- games and activity based materials;

- magic tricks and science toys;

- costumes, hats, and dramatic play props; and

- a display area for books.

Make it obvious that the space is their own by filling it with objects and activities that will interest and stimulate them.

2.2a Emergent and Early Literacy

Six to eight year olds are already focused on reading. It is a major component of their schooling, and they will be aware of their skills or deficiencies in this area. The program should give them a positive environment in which to practice these emerging abilities without focusing on them in a way that will single out overachievers or make struggling readers feel left out. Keep the focus of the program on simple ways to enhance skills. The mix of children in the group will range from the six-year-old emerging reader to the older, more confident reader who can complete simple chapter books. To appeal to this entire age group and reinforce positive literary experiences the focus should be on recreational activities that support cognitive development.

2.2b Pressure-free Reading

Creating an environment in a literature-based program that does not emphasize reading and reading accomplishments is not an easy task. We have been conditioned as teachers, educators, and library programmers to introduce children to the world of reading. Why now, when children are finally beginning to read on their own, would we not be focusing on those skills and abilities? The rationale for not emphasizing reading is based on the fact that school and homework focus great importance on reading, and many children will have preconceived notions of themselves in this arena. They will see themselves as "good" readers or, conversely, as "struggling" readers. They will know where they are in skill and ability in relation to their peers. To reinforce those perceptions in this setting would be counterproductive. Instead, the program needs to focus on literature-based positives. Using literature- and/or theme-based word games and activities with the group will take the focus off reading while allowing time to practice in a pressure-free environment.

2.2c Reading Aloud to Readers

As we have noted, by now most of these children can read and are quite focused on individual reading. Why then would we encourage reading aloud by the programmer? Especially strange, it would seem, is that we would encourage reading *picture* books aloud. We have already established that activities six to eight year olds associate with younger children will be dismissed as babyish. It is our job, then, to ensure that reading aloud is not associated with younger children. Establish right from the beginning that reading aloud is important for everyone, including adults. Grown-ups attend author readings and book clubs. Teens attend poetry readings and listen to music (and pop music's song lyrics are poetry—another form of reading). And people of all ages value self-expression and read aloud from things they have written and composed. Reading aloud to children at this age group is extremely beneficial, and it should be established at the outset of this type of program. Choose titles that are age appropriate and mix up chapter books and picture books and read aloud from both. Developmentally, comprehension and the ability to follow and extend a story are not necessarily tied to individual reading competence. Therefore, both struggling and accomplished readers can share in activities that focus on listening and expanding on a story.

2.2d Books to Share

This is a very exciting age group to choose literature for because they can sit for an extended period of time, allowing you to choose titles that are more involved and have complex plot lines. The choices are virtually limitless: fiction, nonfiction, poetry, and joke books are all suitable choices. Picture books or chapter books are both appropriate, but children at this age enjoy hearing about characters and situations they can relate to. This is an excellent time to introduce complex fairytales or classic tales, especially those that have a notable character as hero or heroine (*Strega Nona,* for example). Choose picture books that stimulate the imagination but focus on children who overcome and accomplish (*Where the Wild Things Are* is a classic example; *Hooway for Wodney Wat* is another good choice). Stories that focus on real situations, especially those that are humorous, are also very popular with this age group (*Clean Your Room, Harvey Moon* for example). If you choose to read "easy readers" aloud to this age group, make sure you are choosing a title for its readability, not its popularity. The books designed for beginning readers will not necessarily stimulate a group when read aloud. Good choices for read-alouds in this genre include *Frog and Toad* and the Henry and Mudge stories. Chapter books are excellent choices to share with a group. You might choose a juvenile novel and read part of it each week over a series of weeks, or you might read an exciting section of a chapter book and encourage children to take it home and have their parents continue the story (be sure to have lots of copies if you choose to highlight an exciting section of a book). There are dozens of books that would be excellent choices for this age group. Some classics that have worked well for us are *Charlie and the Chocolate Factory, The Cricket in Times Square,* and *Ramona the Brave.* Using poetry and joke books is a good technique to help children think of reading in a new and different light. Shel Silverstein's *Where the Sidewalk Ends* is an excellent poetry choice. Joke books come in a wide variety of formats, and most are appropriate for children at this age. You will be limited only by your theme and ability to read without laughing. Reading aloud from joke books should be practiced beforehand, because timing is very important when telling a joke. Of course, you would never read aloud from a book that you hadn't read previously and enjoyed, but taking some extra time with jokes and poetry is important.

2.2e Books to Display

Create an arrangement of books that children might read on their own or take home to have a parent read aloud. Have some books for the younger readers and some for the older audience. Display books that are related to your theme from both the fiction and nonfiction collections. If you are doing an animal theme, for example, choose some simple nonfiction titles about animals. Children will read these if they are interested in learning more about a particular species. Also include picture books, easy readers, and chapter books that focus on animals as characters. Here is a sample of books displayed at a recent animal program for six to eight year olds at our public library:

Giraffes by Julie Murray

Elephants by Jacqueline Dineen

Monkeys and Apes by Barbara Taylor

Five Little Monkeys Wash the Car by Eileen Christelow

Curious George by H. A. Rey

Doctor De Soto Goes to Africa by William Steig

Tacky in Trouble by Helen Lester

Giraffes Can't Dance by Giles Andreae

Cecily G. and the 9 Monkeys by H. A. Rey

A Polar Bear Can Swim: What Animals Can and Cannot Do by Harriet Ziefert

How Big Is Big by Harriet Ziefert

Hand, Hand, Fingers, Thumb by Al Perkins

Animal Jokes compiled and illustrated by Viki Woodworth

Zoodles by Bernard Most

Creature Carnival by Marilyn Singer

A Hippopotamusn't and Other Animal Verses by J. Patrick Lewis

2.2f Reading Incentives

Encouraging children to continue the reading experience at home is a very popular activity for this age group. Children are focused on reading and are quite familiar with practice at home. Therefore, reading incentives should be designed to give a tangible visual mark of individual or group achievement and enhance the fun of coming to the library.

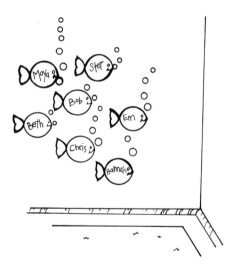

Children will enjoy adding to a visual that is displayed on the wall. Scoops on an ice cream cone, fish in an underwater scene, or animals in the jungle are some typical examples. Use any simple design or die cut to make multiple copies on coloured paper and cut them out. Hand out one to each child. Have children write their names on the shapes, and you (or a parent or caregiver) can write the title of the book they took home from the program. Paste the die cut on the wall and watch the display grow and overflow.

At this age children understand incentives used as part of a game. For example, one programmer designed a reading baseball game. To begin, children take books home and read (individually or with their families). For each book read and returned, children get a "hit" in the game and then draw a baseball card. The card gives them directions to move on an oversize game board. A child might pull a card that reads, "Solid! Run to first base and read a joke book for next week," or "Rain delay! Curl up with your favourite book and read for a while," or "Out of the Park! Home run! You can read anything you'd like . . . you're a star!"

Other incentive-based reading tools that work well with this age group are prize draws. For each book or chapter read the child receives a ticket and enters it for a prize draw. The prize can be just about anything age appropriate. It doesn't need to be expensive or extravagant: publisher give-aways or dollar store treats work well. Children love hearing their names called if they are the winners, and they also enjoy reading and collecting the prize tickets, even if they never win!

3. Programs for Six to Eight Year Olds: Format and Routine

Six to eight year olds are, generally speaking, quite familiar with structured group programming. They are adaptable and flexible when it comes to style and structure. They enjoy having some routine and a predictable set-up, but you don't need to follow a set formula when it comes to programs for this age group. Decide on what you would like to accomplish with your program, find elements that will achieve those goals, and then establish a format that will work for those elements. For example, imagine your goal is to develop a drop-in homework centre where six to eight year olds can come, be supervised, and receive assistance on homework assignments. If the program is running at a public library, ensure that you have sufficient space for tables and chairs, perhaps a computer or two dedicated to research, and staff for supervision and assistance. You can contact local schools and ask to have a flyer announcing the program sent home with children in the appropriate grades. You will need to take emergency contact and other information from interested participants' parents prior to the program's first day. Once the children arrive for their first homework help day, explain your expectations for behaviour and have some extra, library-oriented fun assignments prepared for children who finish their homework before a parent or caregiver arrives to pick them up. Also, you may include a display of age-appropriate books and magazines for participants who finish early. This type of completely open-ended programming works for this age group as long as you are clear about boundaries and behaviour expectations.

In this chapter we provide you with a much more structured set of theme-based programs. These programs are designed as a series of four one-hour programs. Children would be expected to preregister and attend each week for four weeks. This type of formal programming has a very different set of objectives. You will expect children to

- have a positive library experience,

- understand recreational reading and its benefits,

- explore reading and listening comprehension,

- learn to extend stories in artistic and recreational ways, and

- extend the library experience by borrowing books to read at home.

Programs are longer (approximately one hour) and include stories, games, activities, and handicraft projects. The programs are developed as a four week series because it allows time to really explore and develop concepts related to a theme, and it also works really well for seasonal activities. In addition, the children have time to build on the social and peer relationships that six to eight year olds enjoy.

CONFIDENCE BOOSTER

Do literature-based programs need crafts to be successful? Of course not! You can develop a great program with stories interspersed with other activities. However, arts and crafts have the advantage of being open-ended, and children enjoy the freedom of expression. Struggling readers may be intimidated by other aspects of the program but feel comfortable expressing themselves through art. These activities can add value to your program by helping children feel more comfortable and confident.

3.1 Format and Routine

Six to eight year olds enjoy routine and structure, so your program should include patterns that children can expect from week to week. For example, you could begin by having children pick up an identifier they made in the program's first week. Because children can write their own names, you can have them create their own name tags, hats, or buttons to wear each week. Then, after everyone is wearing his or her identifier (the programmer should have one as well), the program can officially begin. If children have come directly after school, you may want to begin with an informal social time that includes a healthy snack. After everyone has gathered a little energy, start the program elements with an introduction to today's activities. If you are building on a concept from a book, begin with the book and follow it with some gross motor activity, perhaps an activity or game. Continue with another project that involves concentration, and so on. As long as the program has a predictable routine and children are allowed the structure that they need to feel comfortable, your program will be successful.

3.2 Variety

Many six to eight year olds will grow bored with a traditional storytime structure (e.g., book, song, rhyme, fingerplay). They are attending a full day of school and have begun to see themselves as "older" children and not "little kids" anymore. They would like their library programs to reflect this. To break the traditional storytime mould and keep children active and interested, your programs should be innovative and have some variety. With this age group it is especially important to stimulate and challenge the children with exciting activities and games. Some children enjoy crafts, others like games, and some like puzzles. Have a variety of elements for your program and keep things moving at a fast pace. Don't be afraid to discard an element that is not working. If you have a group of children that doesn't seem to enjoy crafts, that is, they spend more time chatting than they do painting, switch your focus the following week to games and interactive activities. If you advertised the program's theme prior to registration, then you know participants are interested in the concept. Keep them interested every week by being responsive to their needs and adding some variety.

CONFIDENCE BOOSTER

Include a fun program element that involves reading and writing. Share a silly poem with your group (try collections by Shel Silverstein or Dennis Lee) and then have the children collectively write a funny poem of their own. Ask them to choose a topic and then encourage them to come up with associated words that rhyme. Write the rhyming words on a wipe board or large poster paper. Help them make the words into rhyming phrases. Upon completion, read the silly poem and congratulate your audience of poets.

3.3 Themes

Choosing a theme that will appeal to six to eight year olds is easy because they have such a wide variety of activities and interests. In the next chapter you will find themed programs designed for broad-based appeal. However, you can develop any number of your own by keeping abreast of popular culture, new and noteworthy books, trends, and seasonal activities. Learn about your community and acceptable practices for community members. Some of the themes included in this book may not work for your users if, for example, religious and pagan holidays are not widely accepted. Be sure to tailor your themes and program plans to social customs that will be popular in your area. Strive to avoid bias and provide inclusive services for all members of your community. Introduce children to new things or develop a program based on things that already excite them. When you find a game or activity you like that follows one theme, switch it up, change it, and rearrange it to match another theme. The joy of literature-based programming is that you have a wealth of resources at your fingertips. Think beyond the traditional and expected. Look at things in a new way and keep an open mind. Themes will pop up in the most amazing places. Following are some that have worked in public libraries in recent years.

- **Animation Station:** Junior comics and graphic novels—read some and make your own!

- **Green Thumb Club:** Books on gardening, harvest time, etc., and mini planting projects.

- **Flat Stanley:** Based on the book by Jeff Brown—read and send Flat Stanley around the world.

- **Pet Mania:** Dogs, cats, hamsters, maybe even a degu! Pets are perennial favourites with this age group.

- **Seuss Is on the Loose:** Books, games, and art based on Dr. Seuss titles. The more silly and Seussical the better!

- **Laugh-a-mania:** Jokes, humorous stories, and comedy make for some library-style fun!

- **Only Origami:** Japanese folktales, paper folding books, and a few simple projects make for a program filled with challenging fun.

Just a few ideas to get your mind rolling. Be open and creative and look in places you wouldn't normally expect to find great theme ideas.

3.4 Practice, Practice, Practice

Six to eight year olds enjoy activities they understand and can improve upon. Keep this in mind during your program and allow children to practice and perfect skills and activities. If you play a game that is successful in week one, bring it back again and let children enjoy it a second time. Chances are they will be even better at it when they play it again! Puzzles and complex activities that require steps are also popular with this age group, and giving them a second chance to build on previous successes is a confidence-building approach that children will appreciate and learn from. If you are including vocabulary-building activities in your program (word puzzles, etc.), you might want to pair older and younger children together the first time you try them and then repeat them in a subsequent week with an individual follow-up. Once six to eight year olds understand a concept, they enjoy practicing and perfecting it. Positive reinforcement from you will complete the feeling of success and accomplishment.

4. Programs for Six to Eight Year Olds: Programming Techniques

For this age group your technique should consist of a style and manner that matches your theme and group. Take time to develop your own style and present themes and programs that match it. Never present anything that you don't enjoy. If you're not having fun, the children won't have fun either.

4.1 Recipe for Reading

Read aloud to the children. Use picture books, chapter books, or really good beginning readers. Choose a title that will captivate their imaginations as well as challenge their word recognition and vocabulary-building skills. Set aside part of each week for reading aloud. What if your theme is based on a single story and you read that one in the first week? Add something new, something similar, or something that extends on the story you read the first time. Let's say you are running a Flat Stanley program and you read *Flat Stanley* by Jeff Brown in the first week. The following week read another sophisticated picture book with a memorable character and challenge children to think of ways they could send that character on adventures around the world. Wouldn't Rosemary Well's "Max" and Amelia Bedelia like to travel, too? Reading aloud is so important for children at this age that it is the one step in a program that I would recommend you never, ever skip. Children who are struggling with individual reading may not have time at home to listen to great stories as often as they did when they were preschoolers. Help them keep that magic alive by reading aloud in each and every one of your programs regardless of your format, structure, or theme. (You could even spend some time reading aloud to the children who drop in for help at the homework centre.)

4.2 Individual Expression

Another essential ingredient in programming with six to eight year olds is allowing time for children's self-expression. These children are beginning to rapidly develop their own personalities, outside of their family and moulded by their peers. By giving them time to express themselves through art, writing, drama, and movement you will help them see themselves as individuals. Developing an identity outside of traditional family and friendship circles is a key element for personal growth. Instead of traditional follow-the-leader style activities, have children create their own play or puppet show. Read a chapter of a book and have children paint a picture that represents the next chapter. Play music and encourage children to make up a dance routine. Read some jokes, have children write their own, and then have an "open mike" hour. Expect the unexpected when you encourage open-ended activities. You will build a stockpile of memories, and children will build confidence and individualism.

BRIGHT IDEA

Puppets are a great way for children at this age to express their creativity and imagination. Choose some fairytales and folktalkes from the library's collection that have a minimal number of simple characters and have the children perform plays based on the stories. If they are really enjoying themselves and putting on a good show, you might even want to invite an audience of preschoolers in to watch!

4.3 Games and Participatory Activities

With this age group, you can play a real game! Games with rules, instructions, and a variety of roles are perfect to introduce during programs. Six to eight year olds enjoy order and structure and understand the concept of "playing by the rules." Create games for large groups that match a theme or story. There are a number of simple game styles that you might use to create an activity to match your theme:

- **Trivia game:** Choose simple facts with multiple choice answers, the stranger the fact the better!

- **Secret word:** Create cards with simple, single words that match your theme. Each child takes a turn describing the word on the card without saying it, and the other children try and guess what the word is.

- **Pictionary:** Use dry erase markers and a large wipe board for children to draw pictures matching your theme and have the audience guess the picture.

- **Charades:** A classic game that is perfect for this age group. Be sure to clearly outline the rules (i.e., no speaking, pointing to objects in the room, etc.), because it may be the first time they've played this popular drama game.

- **Matching:** Use clip art to create sets of matching cards, blank on one side and identical in size. Shuffle the cards and lay them out in a grid on the floor with enough room to walk in between. Children take turns and each select two cards, then flip them over to reveal the pictures. The object is to make matches. When a match is revealed the cards remain face up. The game is over when all the cards are overturned.

- **Memory:** Bring in objects that match your theme. Twenty or twenty-five is an ideal number. Arrange them on a table and cover them with a tablecloth. Give each child a blank sheet of paper and a pen and then pull the tablecloth off, revealing the objects for sixty seconds. After the minute is up, cover the objects again and have the children write down everything they can remember.

• **Wall word:** Spell a simple word that matches your theme on 8½-by-11-inch (22-by-28 cm) coloured paper, one letter per sheet. Masking tape the word to the wall with the blank side showing. Children take turns answering questions, and for each correct answer you reveal a letter. The entire group tries to guess the word for a few seconds, then moves on to the next question until someone calls out the correct answer.

> ### BRIGHT IDEA
>
> Create trivia games by using facts that match your theme. The encyclopedia and almanac are great resources for finding exciting factual information. Include multiple choice answers and have children pick their responses by imitating silly actions. For example, if they think the answer is "A," children stand on one foot, for "B" they should put their hands on their heads, and for "C" they can stick out their tongues. Reveal the answer by matching the action!

These are a few of the simple games popular with six to eight year olds. Create others and capitalize on the fact that children at this age enjoy interacting with their friends and playing together using their minds and imaginations.

4.4 Story Extenders

Six to eight year olds have entered a more concrete stage of development. They like realistic things and taking part in real activities. They are less enthusiastic about imaginary characters and pretending, but they can be challenged to create something that will enhance a story they've enjoyed. You could challenge them to create an alternate ending for a short story read aloud, draw a picture of a character from a chapter book, or act out a scene from a picture book or folktale. Six to eight year olds are ready for open-ended, creative challenges. You will be surprised, and frequently amused, at the things they come up with. One favourite accompanies the book *The Gruffalo*. Read the book aloud, keeping the cover hidden, and don't show the pictures. Have children draw their version of the Gruffalo and *then* share the picture from the book.

4.5 Humour

Six to eight year olds can be very funny. They are learning to read and play with their vocabulary. These are the years when children begin to be fascinated with jokes. Use riddles and jokes that match your theme, or add a little comedy to any theme. Let children write, choose, and tell their own jokes. At this age children are especially impressed when they learn how to tell a joke. Be patient with your junior comedians; they are just learning comedy timing and they will often miss and confuse punch lines. Assist them by learning and telling simple jokes of your own. As adults, we are more sophisticated and have gone beyond the obvious puns and simple knock, knock rhythms. These children are just developing a sense of humour that can differentiate and understand double meanings. Synonyms and homonyms are brand new concepts that are both confusing and funny. Include a lighter side in your programs and you will be rewarded with lots of laughter and giggles.

4.6 Incentive-Based Activities

Rewards, prizes, and other tangible outcomes are all techniques that encourage young school-age children to read and participate in reading-based games and activities. Some library traditionalists feel that we should be above bribing children to read by dangling a carrot, in the form of a prize, in front of them. However, contests, give-aways, and other incentives are extremely popular with children and their families. If your goal is to excite children and keep them reading, you may find it useful to use an incentive that lies outside of the simple satisfaction reading brings. Some children do not need incentives to read; they will find pleasure in reading because books unlock their imaginations and take them to places they never imagined. These children will come to the library and read whether you offer incentive-based programs or not. Other children find reading a chore. Six to eight year olds especially can have difficulty reading and have not yet reached a stage of reading for enjoyment. For some children, even the encouragement and dedication of parents and teachers is not enough. For those children, incentive-based reading activities can spark them to rise to the reading challenge. Once they pass over the reading hurdle, they will appreciate the value in reading for the sake of the story. Until that time a prize, sticker, or bookmark might go a long way as an encouragement. In programs, you might ask children to read at home for a period of time each week. Give a prize ticket for every fifteen minutes a child spends reading library books at home. Talk about what they are reading and encourage them to continue. Have bookmarks, stickers, or merit certificates for all the children who don't win the prize.

4.7 Just for Fun

Showing children that reading can be plain and simple fun is a big part of your job in programs for six to eight year olds. Many of these children will find reading difficult and will not want to participate in activities that involve reading or sounding out words. Those children, especially, need to see that reading can be fun. One way to show them is to make library programs fun. If children come to the program and enjoy themselves, they will be comfortable in a setting that promotes reading and literacy, simply through its existence.

Include some elements in your program that have nothing to do with reading. Activities completed just for fun can take some pressure off the children. Games, art activities, and crafts are simple and pleasurable. Relate the activities to your theme and book choices, thereby making positive associations that children will remember.

Make reading *incidental* to some aspects of the program, while modeling reading behaviour. For example, read aloud from a chapter book occasionally. There are no words displayed, and beginning readers don't feel obligated to follow along with the text. Children will enjoy feeling that they are reading "grown-up" books and will allow their imaginations to fill in the pictures. This type of reading is comprehension-based and allows children to enhance that skill. Listening comprehension is often more advanced than children's ability to understand the written word. Children have been listening to words and understanding language since they were a few months old, so it is not surprising that their listening comprehension exceeds their reading ability.

4.8 Peer Interaction

The final word on six to eight year holds has to be friendship. Children are starting to place great importance on relationships and friends. They enjoy interacting, making friends, and developing bonds with other children. Six- and seven-year-old children feel pride at being accepted by the older children, and eight year olds enjoy the sense of seniority that comes with being the oldest in a group. Encourage children to interact and make new friends by pairing them in random twos and threes for games and dividing them in halves for teams. At the upper end of this age range children are beginning to take a sense of ownership of their gender. Some children will only want to make friends with others of the same sex. This is normal and to be expected. However, you will want to make sure registered programs have a number of boys and girls in each program so no one feels left out. Be sensitive to program elements that may seem too "girly" or too "boyish." Just as you don't want children to dismiss an activity as "babyish," you don't want boys to refuse to play a fairy matching game or girls to scoff at reading *The Mouse and His Motorcycle*. Expect the gender defensiveness and come up with creative ways to combat it and break down traditional stereotypes. Have fairies, sprites, and goblins in your game and tell the boys that *The Lord of the Rings* is a book and movie that men love, and it is full of elves, hobbits, and fairy-folk. Remind the girls that motorcycles and trucks are fun for both sexes by using examples from real life of girls and women who enjoy motor sports or drive trucks. Think creatively and be sensitive to this stage of development to make children feel comfortable with their emerging identity but aware that it is okay to break out of the normal gender-based stereotypes.

5. Bibliography of Books to Share

Andreae, Giles. 1999. *Giraffes Can't Dance*. New York: Orchard Books.

Brown, Jeff. 1992. *Flat Stanley*. New York: HarperCollins.

Christelow, Eileen. 2000. *Five Little Monkeys Wash the Car*. Boston: Houghton Mifflin.

Cleary, Beverly. 1965. *The Mouse and the Motorcycle*. New York: William Morrow.

Cleary, Beverly. 1975. *Ramona the Brave*. New York: Morrow.

Cummings, Pat. 1994. *Clean Your Room, Harvey Moon!* New York: Aladdin Publishing Company.

Dahl, Roald. 1973. *Charlie and the Chocolate Factory*. New York: Knopf.

De Paola, Tomie. 1975. *Strega Nona: An Old Tale*. New York: Simon & Schuster Children's Publishing.

Dineen, Jacqueline. 2004. *Elephants*. North Mankato, MN: Smart Apple Media.

Donaldson, Julia. 1999. *The Gruffalo*. London: Macmillan Children's Books.

Lester, Helen. 1998. *Tacky in Trouble*. Boston: Houghton Mifflin.

Lester, Helen. 1999. *Hooway for Wodney Wat*. Boston: Houghton Mifflin.

Lewis, Patrick J. 1990. *A Hippopotamusn't and Other Animal Verses*. New York: Dial Books for Young Readers.

Lobel, Arnold. 1976. *Frog and Toad All Year*. New York: Harper & Row.

Most, Bernard. 1992. *Zoodles*. San Diego: Harcourt Brace Jovanovich.

Murray, Julie. 2002. *Giraffes*. Edina, MN: Abdo Publishing.

Parish, Peggy. 1991. *Amelia Bedelia*. New York: HarperFestival.

Perkins, Al. 1969. *Hand, Hand, Fingers, Thumb*. New York: Random House.

Rey, H. A. 1969. *Cecily G. and the Monkeys*. Boston: Houghton Mifflin.

Rey, H. A. 1969. *Curious George*. Boston: Houghton Mifflin.

Rylant, Cynthia. 1987. *Henry and Mudge: The First Book of Their Adventures*. New York: Bradbury Press.

Selden, George. 1960. *The Cricket in Times Square*. New York: Farrar, Straus & Giroux.

Sendak, Maurice. 1963. *Where the Wild Things Are*. New York: Harper & Row.

Silverstein, Shel. 1974. *Where the Sidewalk Ends: The Poems & Drawings of Shel Silverstein*. New York: HarperCollins.

Singer, Marilyn. 2004. *Creature Carnival*. New York: Hyperion Books for Children.

Steig, William. 1992. *Doctor De Soto Goes to Africa*. New York: HarperCollins.

Taylor, Barbara. 2002. *Monkeys and Apes*. Columbus, OH: Peter Bedrick Books.

Tolkien, J. R. R. 1966. *The Lord of the Rings*. London: HarperCollins.

Wells, Rosemary. 1997. *Bunny Cakes: A Max and Ruby Picture Book*. New York: Dial Books for Young Readers.

Woodworth, Viki. 1993. *Animal Jokes*. Mankato, MN: Child's World.

Ziefert, Harriet. 1995. *How Big Is Big*. Minneapolis, MN: Sagebrush Education Resources.

Ziefert, Harriet. 1998. *A Polar Bear Can Swim: What Animals Can and Cannot Do*. New York: Viking.

Chapter 5

Programs for Six to Eight Year Olds

As we begin our chapter about school-agers, you as a programmer are bound to notice a difference in style, technique, and presentation of the programs that follow. It is a more complex process to program for a six- to eight-year-old group than it was for four and five year olds. School-age children demand more stimulation simply because at this age most children are better equipped mentally and ready to handle slightly more complex information.

Some of the things you'll be able to accomplish with this group are

- reading longer, more thought-provoking books (e.g., *Christmas City* by Michael Garland);

- playing more involved games involving the group as a whole or divided into teams;

- creating more detailed crafts; and

- engaging in more thought-provoking discussions (What does superstition mean? Do you have any?).

Some of the benefits you and your group may obtain follow.

- Group participation—children will ask questions and discuss problems and their solutions.

- Team work—they will develop the ability to work together towards a goal or product.

- Longer attention spans/attentiveness—They will exhibit an eagerness to spend time on the finer details of things, which may work for or against you in some cases if you need to move on to something new or if your program is over.

Also, don't forget to take the time to get to know your group. Ask them questions, find out what they like to read, and try to provide books of interest for future sessions. If you take an interest in the kids, they in return are bound to take an interest in you and what you have to share with them, making your time together an enjoyable experience for everyone!

The following programs follow a four-week plan. We have found this to be beneficial for many reasons:

- The theme covers an entire month at a time.

- Planning is done quickly and easily, allowing for plenty of time to prepare crafts and name tags, to choose books, and to create games if needed.

- Programs can be completed and put together weeks in advance (this is especially beneficial if you or a fellow staff member is absent: the program is completed so there is no last minute scrambling).

Note: Two of the four-week plans that follow are based on holidays or days that are celebrated, such as Halloween and Christmas. It is important to remember that not everyone in your programs will be either celebrating or partaking in any or all of the festivities planned on these days. One way to inform your parents and caregivers of this is to send home a note at the time of registration, advising them of the program theme and what will be happening during those weeks. It is important in your planning to be sensitive to the different ethnicities and cultures in your community.

Let's Get Started!

Our first four-week theme is Creepy Countdown. Why do a whole month on one specific topic? Besides the fact that Halloween is one of the most popular themes to plan for and that kids all over the world love it and celebrate it in different ways (which could be an interesting fact to discuss with your group), this program will show you how having a common theme prepares your group for the weeks ahead. They will know every week what types of stories, books, and games they will be involved with. Parents and caregivers also will know exactly what topic will be focused on for the entire session, making it easier for them to decide whether or not they want their child(ren) to participate.

Six to Eight Year Olds: Creepy Countdown

The following programs contain enough stories, games, and activities to cover a one-hour session with your group. Every week should begin in the same way. A typical one-hour session would be planned and implemented in the following manner:

- **Hand out name tags**—Handing them out each week by calling the children up to get them, instead of having them on the table for the children to pick up themselves, helps you to learn the children's names more quickly.

  Time Frame—5 minutes

- **Great Game:** *Hangman*—*Hangman* is a game that focuses on building literacy, phonics, and spelling skills. Children take turns guessing missing letters of a word, question, or phrase until all of the letters are filled and the word or phrase can be read in its entirety. Follow this up with a brief discussion (e.g., Superstition—what does that mean?).

  Time Frame—10 minutes

- **Story**—Try to include a story that will follow up on or tie together the main theme of the program.

  Time Frame—5 minutes

- **Crafty Creation**—Show your example to give the children a brief understanding of what they will be making. Be careful not to give too many instructions (if there are quite a few) to begin with. If the craft requires a lot of explanation, do it one step at a time so the group doesn't become confused. The Crafty Creation is done towards the beginning of the program to allow time for drying if needed.

  Time Frame—15 minutes

- **Awesome Activity**—This is the best opportunity to get the children moving and thinking after sitting during the beginning of the program.

  Time Frame—10 minutes

- **Story/Video**—Gather the group together and use the last few minutes to read a final story or watch a short video. Don't forget to remind the children that there are books available for borrowing or browsing.

  Time Frame—7 minutes

- **Choosing a story and dismissal**—Let the group browse through the books you have chosen to display. Once students have chosen a book (or not), they can then be dismissed.

  Time Frame—3 minutes

Six to Eight Year Olds: Week 1—Creepy Countdown

Books to Share

A Creepy Countdown by Charlotte Huck

The House That Drac Built by Judy Sierra

Fright Night Flight by Laura Krauss Melmed

Great Game

Hangman Phrase: Welcome to Creepy Countdown

How to Play:

1. Think of a word or phrase (e.g., superstition).

2. Using a dry-erase or chalkboard, draw dashes to represent the letters. (e.g., _ _ _ _ _ _ _).

3. Have children take turns guessing letters of the alphabet that they think could be in the word(s).

4. If a letter in the word is guessed correctly, that letter is filled in the appropriate space(s). If a letter is guessed incorrectly, a part of a stick figure person is drawn on the board (head, body, arm, leg, etc.).

5. The object of the game is to guess the word or phrase before the entire stick figure is drawn on the board.

Awesome Activity

Interesting Icebreaker: Hallowe'en Who/What Am I?

Getting started: Photocopy or draw enough Hallowe'en pictures, approximately 2-by-2-inches/ 5-by-5 cm in size, for your group. Ideas are listed below. Cut them out and back them onto construction or any paper to make cards approximately 3-by-3-inches in size. Colour the pictures if needed and laminate them to ensure that they will be reusable.

When you are ready to play: Explain the object of the game and rules to remember, listed below, to the group and then proceed to tape a picture onto the back of each player. This should be done in a way that enables every player (except the one the picture is taped to) to see what person or object each player is. The game begins when every player has a card taped to his or her back. The game ends when all players have figured out who or what objects they are.

From Beth Maddigan and Stefanie Drennan, *The BIG Book of Reading, Rhyming, and Resources: Programs for Children Ages 4-8*. Westport, CT: Libraries Unlimited. © 2005.

Six to Eight Year Olds: Week 1—Creepy Countdown

Object of the game: Players move around the room asking questions of other players to try to gather hints about who or what they are.

Rules to remember:

- **Questions**—Questions asked by players must be answerable by "yes" or "no" only (e.g., Do I have wings? Do I fly? Do I have two feet? Am I an animal?).

- **Players who finish early**—Players who are able to figure out their cards early may continue to answer questions for those still playing.

- **Hints**—Players may give small hints to each other if one or more are stumped but must be careful not to give too much away.

Six to Eight Year Olds:
Week 1—Creepy Countdown

Crafty Creation

Jack-on-a-Plate

Handy Hint 1—Use sponges to dab the paint on the paper plate to give a different effect. Buy them at your local dollar or discount store and cut them in half or into four squares.

Handy Hint 2—If you don't have the room to store the crafts until the following week, you may wish to explain to the group ahead of time to use the paint sparingly. The more paint they use, the longer it will take for their craft to dry.

Materials

Large paper plates—1 per child

Paint sticks/stirrers—1 per child

Green construction paper

Brown construction paper

Orange tempera paint

Glue sticks

Paint brushes or sponges

Scissors

Black markers

Masking tape

Exacto knife—This should be used only by the programmer/adults present and should be kept well out of the children's reach.

Instructions

1. Draw two triangular eyes at the top of the paper plate (so that if you hold it up to your face, you can see through the eyes) and using the Exacto knife, cut out the eyes. Continue to do this to all of the plates you will be using in your program.

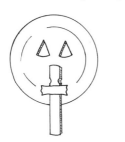

2. Using masking tape, tape a paint stick onto the back of each plate. These are the handles for the masks.

From Beth Maddigan and Stefanie Drennan, *The BIG Book of Reading, Rhyming, and Resources: Programs for Children Ages 4-8*. Westport, CT: Libraries Unlimited. © 2005.

Six to Eight Year Olds:
Week 1—Creepy Countdown

3.   Paint the paper plate orange and let it dry (this can be done by the children at the beginning of your program).

4.   Using the brown construction paper, cut enough rectangles (approximately 2-by-3-inch/ 5-by-7 cm in size) for your group. These are the stems. Glue one in the center at the top of each plate.

5.   Using the green construction paper, cut out circles of various sizes. Then using your scissors, cut into the circles and continue to cut until you have a coil. These are the vines. Glue them anywhere on the plate.

6.   Provide the children with black markers so that they can draw on the pumpkin noses and mouths themselves to really give Jack a personality.

From Beth Maddigan and Stefanie Drennan, *The BIG Book of Reading, Rhyming, and Resources: Programs for Children Ages 4-8*. Westport, CT: Libraries Unlimited. © 2005.

Six to Eight Year Olds: Week 2—Creepy Countdown

Books to Share

If You Were Really Superstitious by Jane Sarnoff

Knock on Wood: Poems about Superstitions by Janet S. Wong

The Follower by Richard Thompson

Great Game

Hangman Phrase: Are You Superstitious?

Discuss superstitions and superstitious behaviours with your group using some of the examples of silly superstitions found in *If You Were Really Superstitious* by Jane Sarnoff. Start by asking your group what "superstitious" means and follow with examples. While not all of the superstitions are suitable for discussion, there are quite a few that are sure to make your group giggle.

How to Play:

1. Think of a word or phrase (e.g., superstition).

2. Using a dry-erase or chalkboard, draw dashes to represent the letters. (e.g., _ _ _ _ _ _ _).

3. Have children take turns guessing letters of the alphabet that they think could be in the word(s).

4. If a letter in the word is guessed correctly, that letter is filled in the appropriate space(s). If a letter is guessed incorrectly, a part of a stick figure person is drawn on the board (head, body, arm, leg, etc.).

5. The object of the game is to guess the word or phrase before the entire stick figure is drawn on the board.

Awesome Activity

Witch's Broomstick

This game is played similar to *Hot Potato*. You can either use music or simply say the chant as you play. It goes like this:

Pass the witch's broomstick all around the room,

While the music plays you must quickly pass the broom.

Anyone is out who lets the broomstick drop,

Or the one who's holding it when the music stops!

Getting started: All you need is a broomstick.

From Beth Maddigan and Stefanie Drennan, *The BIG Book of Reading, Rhyming, and Resources: Programs for Children Ages 4-8*. Westport, CT: Libraries Unlimited. © 2005.

Six to Eight Year Olds:
Week 2—Creepy Countdown

When you are ready to play: Explain the object of the game as well as the rules to remember to your group. Next, have your group stand in a circle and while the chant is being said, pass a broomstick very quickly around the circle.

Object of the game: If the broomstick is dropped, the person who dropped it is out. Whoever has it when the word "stops" is said is also out. You can either send the players who are out to the middle of the circle for the next round only or keep adding to the middle and play until there is only one person left standing.

Rules to remember: Both of each player's hands must touch the broomstick as it is passed to the next player.

Six to Eight Year Olds:
Week 2—Creepy Countdown

Crafty Creation

Ghost-of-a-Time Windsock

Materials

White poster board (4 strips per sheet)—enough for your group

Tissue paper strips—various colours

String or yarn

Masking tape

Hole punch

Glue sticks

Decorating materials—markers, crayons, glitter

Instructions

1. Cut a sheet of poster board into four long strips.

2. Cut tissue paper into streamers 24 inches/60 cm long.

3. Cut yarn into pieces 12 inches/30 cm long (one per ghost).

4. Have the children draw the ghost's face, and using a glue stick, attach streamers to the inside of the ghost's head. (To do this, they will need to put the ghost face down on the table in front of them.)

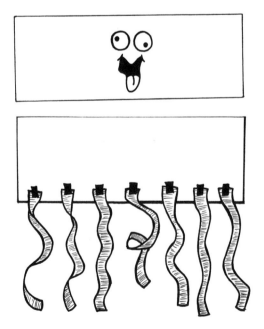

From Beth Maddigan and Stefanie Drennan, *The BIG Book of Reading, Rhyming, and Resources: Programs for Children Ages 4-8*. Westport, CT: Libraries Unlimited. © 2005.

112

Six to Eight Year Olds:
Week 2—Creepy Countdown

5. Once the decorating is complete, join the ends of the poster board to form a cylinder and secure in place using masking tape.

6. Punch a hole on the left and right sides of the ghost (near the top) and tie the yarn on to form both the handle to carry it and the string to hang it with.

Six to Eight Year Olds:
Week 3—Creepy Countdown

Books to Share

The Spider and the Fly by Mary Howitt

Mystery Mansion: A Look Again Book by Michael Garland

Room on the Broom by Julia Donaldson

Great Game

Hangman Phrase: What Will You Be for Hallowe'en?

How to Play:

1. Think of a word or phrase (e.g., superstition).
2. Using a dry-erase or chalkboard, draw dashes to represent the letters. (e.g., _ _ _ _ _ _ _).
3. Have children take turns guessing letters of the alphabet that they think could be in the word(s).
4. If a letter in the word is guessed correctly, that letter is filled in the appropriate space(s). If a letter is guessed incorrectly, a part of a stick figure person is drawn on the board (head, body, arm, leg, etc.).
5. The object of the game is to guess the word or phrase before the entire stick figure is drawn on the board.

Awesome Activity

Count Spookula

Getting started: Explain the object of the game and the rules to remember, listed below, to your entire group.

When you are ready to play: Have your entire group stand shoulder to shoulder in a circle and close their eyes. While their eyes are closed, circle them in silence and choose the Count by tapping one of the children on the shoulder. This child will be the Count for this game.

The game begins on the word go, and children must break away from the circle and begin introducing themselves to one another. They must always shake hands with anyone they meet and say " Hi, my name is _____." The other person then introduces himself or herself in the same way. After they introduce themselves they may say a few parting words but must move on to someone new and introduce themselves again. Count Spookula will introduce himself or herself the same way as all of the others with one exception: He or she will use the index finger of

From Beth Maddigan and Stefanie Drennan, *The BIG Book of Reading, Rhyming, and Resources: Programs for Children Ages 4-8*. Westport, CT: Libraries Unlimited. © 2005.

Six to Eight Year Olds:
Week 3—Creepy Countdown

the hand he or she is shaking with to tap the inside of the prey's wrist (like pointing backwards towards the person). The prey now must continue to walk around and introduce himself or herself but must also count to 10 silently. Once 8 or 9 is reached the prey must act sleepy and by 10 he or she must sit on the floor.

Object of the game: Count Spookula must try to put the entire group to sleep without anyone figuring out who he or she is.

Rules to remember: If you think you know who the Count is you are allowed to guess but must say the following phrase out loud: "Hark! It's not a lark. . . . It's Count Spookula!" BUT . . . there is a catch . . . choosing incorrectly will put you to sleep also.

From Beth Maddigan and Stefanie Drennan, *The BIG Book of Reading, Rhyming, and Resources: Programs for Children Ages 4-8*. Westport, CT: Libraries Unlimited. © 2005.

Six to Eight Year Olds:
Week 3—Creepy Countdown

Be-Witching Candy Cups!

Handy Hint—Tape the cups together ahead of time so that your group can get right to crafting.

Materials

Small Styrofoam cups—3 per child

Permanent markers—thick tipped—various colors or black—enough for your group

Black construction paper

Green construction paper

Liquid paper

Masking tape

Glue sticks

Instructions

1. Using masking tape, tape two of the Styrofoam cups together at the rim. This will be the witch's body.

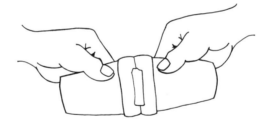

2. Cut two 5-by-3-inch/13-by-8 cm strips from black construction paper (measurements don't have to be exact) and roll each strip around a pencil or marker to make a cylinder for the arm.

3. Cut simple hand (mitten) shapes out of green construction paper. Put a piece of tape on one of the hands and insert it into the arm. Repeat with the other arm.

4. Flatten the other end of the arm (the end without the hand) and tape it to the top of the cups that you taped together. Repeat with the other arm.

From Beth Maddigan and Stefanie Drennan, *The BIG Book of Reading, Rhyming, and Resources: Programs for Children Ages 4-8*. Westport, CT: Libraries Unlimited. © 2005.

5. Cut a small 2-by-2-inch/5-by-5 cm square out of green construction paper and set aside.

6. Trace a small construction paper plate onto black construction paper, cut it out, and set it aside. (This is the hat rim.)

7. Trace a second circle (same size) onto black construction paper and cut it out. Cut a slit to the middle point of the circle, roll the circle into a cone, and tape it in place. (This is the top of the hat.) Tape the cone onto the rim to make the witch's hat. Set it aside.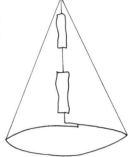

8. Cut the last cup in half and throw away the top portion (all you need is the bottom part). Colour this black as well.

9. Once you have coloured your entire witch black (or whatever color you choose), take the green square (from step 5) and draw the witch's face onto it. Using a glue stick glue this onto the top cup (the one cut in half).

10. Using a glue stick, attach the last cup (rim up) on top of the body (to cover where the arms have been taped on).

From here you have two choices:

1. Using a glue stick, line the rim of the top Styrofoam cup and gently place the hat on top. Push down gently to get the hat to adhere to the cup.

2. Do not glue the hat on and use your witch as a candy holder.

Once this activity is finished, discuss with your group what costumes they are planning to wear for Hallowe'en. This would be a great time to discuss Halloween and costume customs in other countries as well as how the custom of Halloween itself got started. Look for books such as *Hallowe'en: Why We Celebrate It the Way We Do* to give you a head start. They are filled with fun and interesting facts that you will want to share.

From Beth Maddigan and Stefanie Drennan, *The BIG Book of Reading, Rhyming, and Resources: Programs for Children Ages 4-8*. Westport, CT: Libraries Unlimited. © 2005.

Six to Eight Year Olds:
Week 4—Creepy Countdown

Books to Share

Catmagic by Loris Lesynski

Scary, Scary Halloween by Eve Bunting

By the Light of the Halloween Moon by Caroline Stutson

Great Game

Hangman Phrase: Have a Safe and Happy Hallowe'en!

How to Play:

1. Think of a word or phrase (e.g., superstition).
2. Using a dry-erase or chalkboard, draw dashes to represent the letters. (e.g., _ _ _ _ _ _ _).
3. Have children take turns guessing letters of the alphabet that they think could be in the word(s).
4. If a letter in the word is guessed correctly, that letter is filled in the appropriate space(s). If a letter is guessed incorrectly, a part of a stick figure person is drawn on the board (head, body, arm, leg, etc.).
5. The object of the game is to guess the word or phrase before the entire stick figure is drawn on the board.

Awesome Activity

Spider's Web

Getting started: To begin, you'll need a large ball of yarn. Explain the rules to remember and object of the game (listed below) to your group.

When you're ready to play: Have your group stand facing each other in a circle. Give the ball of yarn to one of the children and instruct him or her to toss it to someone else in the circle, who must then wrap it once around his or her waist and toss it to someone else. This continues until the entire ball of yarn is gone. The person left holding the end of the yarn must then start the un-tangling process.

Object of the game: The entire group must work together to get themselves free of the spider's web.

Rules to remember: The web must be untangled one person at a time. Once one person is free, he or she must then work to untangle the next person, and so on.

Six to Eight Year Olds:
Week 4—Creepy Countdown

Going Batty!

Handy Hint—*Have some Hallowe'en treats on hand to send home with your group in these fun containers. Ask parents/caregivers before giving out food to a group of children. Children may have food allergies or sensitivities that can be dangerous.*

Materials

Empty (and washed out) 2 litre (half gallon) juice boxes—1 per child

Black construction paper

White card stock—½ sheet per person

Glue sticks

Scissors

Decorating materials—glitter, stickers (optional), markers

Instructions

1. Fold an 8½-by-11-inch/22-by-28 cm piece of black construction paper in half lengthwise and cut along the crease. This will give you two long pieces.

2. Fold the two long pieces in half (giving you a rectangle shape) and cut along the fold. This will give you four black rectangles.

3. Place one black rectangle lengthwise, matching it up with the bottom of a juice carton, and mark a line where it ends with a pencil.

4. Using an Exacto knife, cut off the top of the juice carton (down to where the pencil line is).

5. Using a glue stick, glue the rectangles onto the four sides of the juice carton to cover it.

From Beth Maddigan and Stefanie Drennan, *The BIG Book of Reading, Rhyming, and Resources: Programs for Children Ages 4-8*. Westport, CT: Libraries Unlimited. © 2005.

Six to Eight Year Olds:
Week 4—Creepy Countdown

6. Photocopy, trace onto black construction paper, and cut out the wing templates. Glue them onto the back (see illustration).

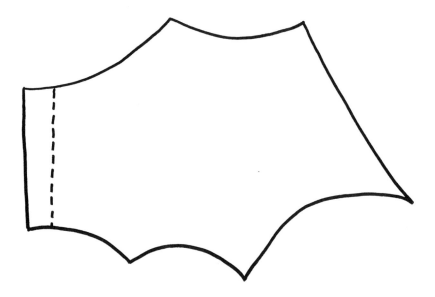

7. Cut a strip of black construction paper about 10 inches/25 cm long and glue it to the outside of the container (this is your handle).

8. Using the ear template, cut 3-by-3-by-inch triangles out of black construction paper and glue them to the top of the carton.

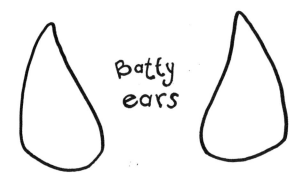

Batty ears

Six to Eight Year Olds:
Week 4—Creepy Countdown

9. Photocopy the eye and eyebrow and fang templates and cut out enough for everyone (using white cardstock) or let the children create their own. Give them white paper, scissors, and markers and let them get creative.

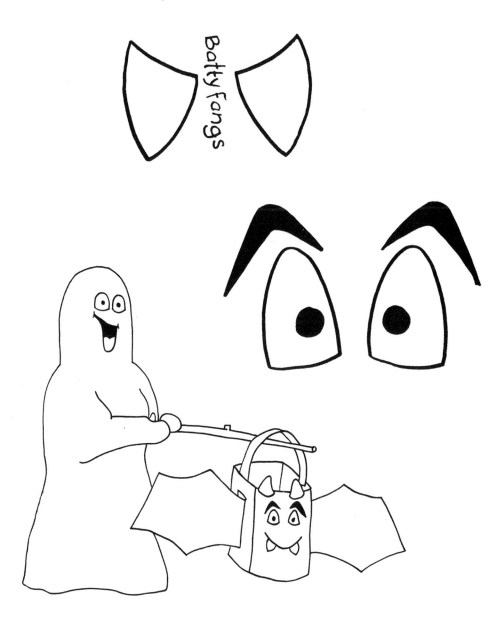

Six to Eight Year Olds: Christmas Creations

Let's Get Started!

Welcome to the next theme in this chapter: Christmas Creations. With the abundance of materials available on Christmas and Christmas celebrations, these next four weeks are a snap to plan. Be sure to take some time to discuss the different traditions celebrated around the world as well as those celebrated by the children in your classroom or library group. Some great books to get you started are: *Christmas Around the World* by Mary D. Lankford and *Children Around the World Celebrate Christmas* by Susan T. Osborn. The children in your group will delight in hearing how holiday celebrations differ from country to country and home to home.

From Beth Maddigan and Stefanie Drennan, *The BIG Book of Reading, Rhyming, and Resources: Programs for Children Ages 4-8*. Westport, CT: Libraries Unlimited. © 2005.

Six to Eight Year Olds: Christmas Creations

The following programs contain enough stories, games, and activities to cover a one-hour session with your group. Every week should begin in the same way. A typical one-hour session would be planned and implemented in the following manner:

- **Hand out name tags**—Handing them out each week by calling the children up to get them, instead of having them on the table for the children to pick up themselves, helps you to learn the children's names more quickly.

  Time Frame—5 minutes

- **Great Game: *Snowman***—*Snowman,* like *Hangman,* is a game that focuses on building literacy, phonics, and spelling skills. Children take turns guessing missing letters of a word, question, or phrase until all of the letters are filled and the word or phrase can be read in its entirety. Follow this up with a brief discussion (e.g., What will you do on Christmas morning?).

  Time Frame—10 minutes

- **Story**—Try to include a story that will follow up on or tie together the main theme of the program.

  Time Frame—5 minutes

- **Crafty Creation**—Show your example to give the children a brief understanding of what they will be making. Be careful not to give too many instructions (if there are quite a few) to begin with. If the craft requires a lot of explanation, do it one step at a time so the group doesn't get confused. The Crafty Creation is done toward the beginning of the program to allow time for drying if needed.

  Time Frame—15 minutes

- **Awesome Activity**—This is the best opportunity to get the children moving and thinking after sitting during the beginning of the program.

  Time Frame—10 minutes

- **Story/Video**—Gather the group together and use the last few minutes to read a final story or watch a short video. Don't forget to remind the children that there are books available for borrowing or browsing.

  Time Frame—7 minutes

- **Choosing a story and dismissal**—Let the group browse through the books you have chosen to display. Once they have chosen a book (or not), they can then be dismissed.

  Time Frame—3 minutes

From Beth Maddigan and Stefanie Drennan, *The BIG Book of Reading, Rhyming, and Resources: Programs for Children Ages 4-8*. Westport, CT: Libraries Unlimited. © 2005.

Six to Eight Year Olds:
Week 1—Christmas Creations

Books to Share

Snowmen at Night by Caralyn Buehner
Peter Claus and the Naughty List by Lawrence David
Olive, the Orphan Reindeer by Michael Christie

Great Game

Snowman Phrase: Welcome to Christmas Creations

How to Play:

1. Think of a word or phrase (e.g., traditions).
2. Using a dry-erase or chalkboard, draw dashes to represent the letters. (e.g., _ _ _ _ _ _ _ _ _ _).
3. Have children take turns guessing letters of the alphabet that they think could be in the word(s).
4. If a letter in the word is guessed correctly, that letter is put in the appropriate space(s). If a letter is guessed incorrectly, a part of a snowman is drawn on the board (head, hat, arm, broom, etc.).
5. The object of the game is to guess the word or phrase before the entire snowman is drawn on the board.

Awesome Activity

Santa's Sack

Getting started: You will need:

- 2 small cloth bags or sacks (that you cannot see through)
- Individually wrapped candies (enough for your group)
- 2 dice (one for each team)

Before you begin, divide the candies in half and put one half in each bag.

When you are ready to play: Divide your group into two teams and have them sit in two lines facing the same direction (one behind the other). The people in front get a sack and a die to begin. When one of them gets a six, Santa's Sack is passed, along with the die, to the person sitting behind him or her, who then tries to get a six to pass the sack, and so on.

Objective: The team who gets their sack to the end of their line first wins. Once this game is over you can either play again or open the sack and let each team member have a reward for a game well played!

Ask parents/caregivers before giving out food to a group of children. Children may have food allergies or sensitivities that can be dangerous.

From Beth Maddigan and Stefanie Drennan, *The BIG Book of Reading, Rhyming, and Resources: Programs for Children Ages 4-8*. Westport, CT: Libraries Unlimited. © 2005.

Six to Eight Year Olds:
Week 1—Christmas Creations

Crafty Creation

Puzzle Piece Picture Frame

Handy Hint 1—*This craft should be done at the beginning of the program so that the paint has enough time to dry before the children take their masterpieces home.*

Handy Hint 2—*Using three puzzle pieces, make a reindeer decoration to glue onto the corner of your frame. Take a wide puzzle piece (this is the face of the reindeer) and glue two thinner pieces on the left and right corners (these are the antlers) Glue on two small wiggle eyes and, using a red marker, draw on a nose. See illustration.*

Materials

Cereal Boxes—1 box per 4 children

Old puzzle pieces—approximately 15 pieces per child

Glue sticks

Small sponges—1 per child

Tempera washable paint—red and green

Glitter—optional

Exacto knife—This should be used only by the programmer/adults present and should be kept well out of the children's reach.

Instructions

1. Trace a 4-by-5-inch/10-by-13 cm photo onto a cereal box. Using a ruler, draw a 2-inch/ 5 cm border around the photo rectangle.

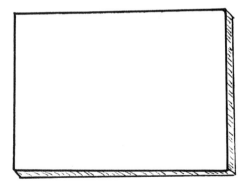

Six to Eight Year Olds:
Week 1—Christmas Creations

2. Cut out the large rectangle and, using an Exacto knife, cut out the 4-by-5-inch/10-by-13 cm photo rectangle. This is your picture frame.

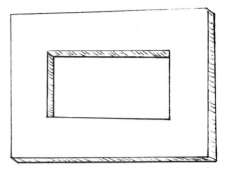

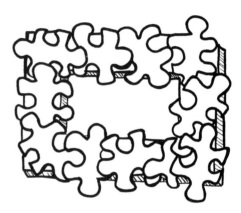

3. Using a glue stick, glue puzzle pieces in any pattern around the frame.

4. Using a small sponge, dab red and green paint on the frame (enough to cover the pieces and frame without leaving any large globs that won't dry in time).

5. Using the sponge, dab glitter onto the wet paint. Let dry.

From Beth Maddigan and Stefanie Drennan, *The BIG Book of Reading, Rhyming, and Resources: Programs for Children Ages 4-8*. Westport, CT: Libraries Unlimited. © 2005.

Six to Eight Year Olds:
Week 2—Christmas Creations

The Polar Express by Chris Van Allsburg
Christmas City by Michael Garland
Santa's New Suit by Laura Rader

Great Game

Snowman Phrase: What Is Your Christmas Wish?

How to Play:

1. Think of a word or phrase (e.g., traditions).
2. Using a dry-erase or chalkboard, draw dashes to represent the letters. (e.g., _ _ _ _ _ _ _ _ _ _).
3. Have children take turns guessing letters of the alphabet that they think could be in the word(s).
4. If a letter in the word is guessed correctly, that letter is put in the appropriate space(s). If a letter is guessed incorrectly, a part of a snowman is drawn on the board (head, hat, arm, broom, etc.).
5. The object of the game is to guess the word or phrase before the entire snowman is drawn on the board.

Note: Read the story *The Polar Express* after doing the following activity.

Awesome Activity

The Right Family Christmas Story

Christmas was almost here and Mother RIGHT was finishing the Christmas baking. Father RIGHT, Susie RIGHT, and Billy RIGHT returned from their last minute Christmas errands. "There's not much LEFT to be done," said Father RIGHT as he came into the kitchen. "Did you leave the basket of food at the church?" asked Mother RIGHT. "I LEFT it RIGHT where you told me to," said Billy RIGHT. "I don't have any money LEFT." The hall telephone rang and Susie RIGHT LEFT to answer it. She rushed back and told the family, "Aunt Tillie RIGHT LEFT a package for us RIGHT on Grandma RIGHT'S porch. I'll go over there RIGHT now and get it," she said as she LEFT in a rush. Father RIGHT LEFT the kitchen and went to bring in the Christmas tree. By the time Susie RIGHT returned, Mother RIGHT, Father RIGHT, and Billy RIGHT had begun trimming the tree. The entire RIGHT family sang Christmas carols as they finished the decorating. Then they LEFT all the presents arranged under the tree and went to bed, hoping that they had selected the RIGHT gifts for their family. Now I hope that you have the RIGHT present for yourself, because that's all that's LEFT of our story, except to wish you all a Merry Christmas, isn't that RIGHT?

Getting started: You will need:

- Small bells (found at any local craft or dollar store)
- Yarn, any colour

From Beth Maddigan and Stefanie Drennan, *The BIG Book of Reading, Rhyming, and Resources: Programs for Children Ages 4-8*. Westport, CT: Libraries Unlimited. © 2005.

Six to Eight Year Olds:
Week 2—Christmas Creations

Cut the yarn in pieces 24 inches/60 cm long. Lace one end through the loop on the bell and tie the two ends closed to make necklaces that jingle. Make enough of these for your group.

Wrap each necklace in a couple of layers of tissue paper and tape closed securely.

When you're ready to play: Everyone stands in a circle holding one of the wrapped packages containing the necklaces. The programmer reads the story (above), and every time the word RIGHT is read, everyone passes his or her package to the right. Every time the word LEFT is read, packages are passed to the left. The package that each person is holding at the end of the story is the one he or she opens and gets to keep.

Object of the game: A fun activity to help introduce the next story to be read aloud.

Six to Eight Year Olds: Week 2—Christmas Creations

Crafty Creation

Rudolph's Reindeer Box

Handy Hint—Have some Christmas treats (candy canes, chocolate kisses, jelly beans) on hand to send home with your group in these fun containers. Ask parents/caregivers before giving out food to a group of children. Children may have food allergies or sensitivities that can be dangerous.

Materials

Empty (and washed out) 2 litre (half gallon) juice boxes—1 per child

Brown construction paper

Card stock

Glue sticks

Scissors

Large red pom-poms—1 per child

Decorating materials—glitter, stickers (optional), markers

Exacto knife—This should be used only by the programmer/adults present and should be kept well out of the children's reach.

Instructions

1. Fold an 8½-by-11-inch/22-by-28 cm piece of brown construction paper in half lengthwise and cut along the crease. This will give you two long pieces.

2. Fold the two long pieces in half (giving you a rectangle shape) and cut along the fold. This will give you four brown rectangles.

3. Place one brown rectangle lengthwise, matching it up with the bottom of a juice carton, and mark a line where it ends with a pencil.

4. Using an Exacto knife, cut off the top of the juice carton (down to where the pencil line is)

5. Using a glue stick, glue the rectangles onto the four sides of the juice carton to cover it.

Six to Eight Year Olds:
Week 2—Christmas Creations

6. Photocopy (and enlarge), trace onto brown construction paper, and cut out the antler templates. Glue them onto the back (see illustration).

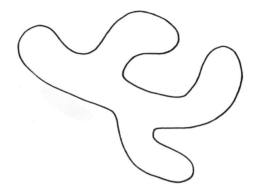

7. Cut a strip of brown construction paper about 10 inches/25 cm long and glue it to the outside of the container (this is your handle).

8. Photocopy the ear and eyebrow templates and back them onto cardstock to make tracers. Trace them onto brown construction paper and cut out the antlers.

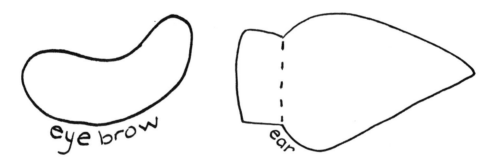

9. Place all of the pieces needed inside the carton for the children to glue on with a glue stick (including the large red pom-pom nose).

10. Provide markers for the children to draw eyes and a mouth on the carton when they are finished.

From Beth Maddigan and Stefanie Drennan, *The BIG Book of Reading, Rhyming, and Resources: Programs for Children Ages 4-8*. Westport, CT: Libraries Unlimited. © 2005.

Six to Eight Year Olds:
Week 3—Christmas Creations

Books to Share

Santa Claustrophobia by Mike Reiss

How Murray Saved Christmas by Mike Reiss

Who'll Pull Santa's Sleigh Tonight? by Laura Rader

Great Game

Snowman Phrase: What Will You Do on Christmas Morning?

How to Play:

1. Think of a word or phrase (e.g., traditions).

2. Using a dry-erase or chalkboard, draw dashes to represent the letters. (e.g., _ _ _ _ _ _ _ _ _ _).

3. Have children take turns guessing letters of the alphabet that they think could be in the word(s).

4. If a letter in the word is guessed correctly, that letter is put in the appropriate space(s). If a letter is guessed incorrectly, a part of a snowman is drawn on the board (head, hat, arm, broom, etc.).

5. The object of the game is to guess the word or phrase before the entire snowman is drawn on the board.

Awesome Activity

Christmas Carol Chaos

Getting started: What you'll need:

- Pad of paper and marker for each group

When you are ready to play: Divide your group into two teams and have them come up with a "Christmassy" team name (e.g., Santa's Little Helpers). Each team sends one player up to the Game Master (programmer), who gives them the name of a popular Christmas song or carol. The player then returns to the group and tries to get the group to guess the name of the carol by drawing only. As soon as the group knows the song, they must sing it as loud as they can. After singing, they send a new person for another song. Play continues until one group completes five songs.

From Beth Maddigan and Stefanie Drennan, *The BIG Book of Reading, Rhyming, and Resources: Programs for Children Ages 4-8*. Westport, CT: Libraries Unlimited. © 2005.

Six to Eight Year Olds:
Week 3—Christmas Creations

Object of the game: To be the first team to figure out and begin to sing the Christmas carols.

Rules to remember: If the name of your Christmas carol contains more than one word, you can let your group write down a word in the title once it is said by someone in the group, until they get the whole title.

Some Christmas carols that would be fun and easy to draw and sing are

"Jingle Bells,"

"Rudolph the Red Nosed Reindeer,"

"Frosty the Snowman," and

"Santa Claus Is Coming to Town."

From Beth Maddigan and Stefanie Drennan, *The BIG Book of Reading, Rhyming, and Resources: Programs for Children Ages 4-8*. Westport, CT: Libraries Unlimited. © 2005.

Six to Eight Year Olds:
Week 3—Christmas Creations

O' Advent Tree

Materials

Green poster board—1 sheet per child

Resealable storage bags—1 per child

Masking tape

Yellow construction paper—½ sheet per child

Red construction paper—2 sheets per child

Black marker

Hole punch

String—any colour

Decorating materials—glitter, stickers

Instructions

1. Fold a large sheet of green poster board in half and open it back up.

2. Using a glue stick, cover ½ of the poster board in glue and fold it over. Press down to make the two sides adhere.

3. Draw a large Christmas tree shape on the poster board and cut it out.

4. Using a hole punch, punch a hole near the top of the tree.

From Beth Maddigan and Stefanie Drennan, *The BIG Book of Reading, Rhyming, and Resources: Programs for Children Ages 4-8*. Westport, CT: Libraries Unlimited. © 2005.

133

Six to Eight Year Olds:
Week 3—Christmas Creations

5. Cut a piece of string 6 inches/15 cm in length and loop it through the hole. Tie a knot in the ends. This is what you will hang the tree with.

6. Photocopy (and enlarge) the circle template, then use it to trace circles onto red construction paper and cut them out. Each child will need twenty-five circles.

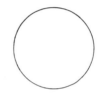

7. Using a black marker, write the numbers from 1 to 25 on the red circles and place them in a resealable plastic bag. Using masking tape, tape the bags onto the backs of the trees. These are the counters for counting down to Christmas. Starting on the first day of December, the children will tape or glue one red circle on each day until Christmas day.

8. Photocopy (and enlarge) and cut out the star template. Trace the star onto yellow construction paper and cut out one star per child.

9. Explain how an advent tree works and let the children decorate it with glitter, stickers, or markers.

10. Finish the tree by gluing the star on top.

Six to Eight Year Olds:
Week 4—Christmas Creations

Books to Share

Mr. Willowby's Christmas Tree by Robert Barry

The Night Before Christmas by Jan Brett

The Mouse Before Christmas by Michael Garland

Great Game

Snowman Phrase: Have a Very Merry Christmas and a Happy New Year!

How to Play:

1. Think of a word or phrase (e.g., traditions).

2. Using a dry-erase or chalkboard, draw dashes to represent the letters. (e.g., _ _ _ _ _ _ _ _ _ _).

3. Have children take turns guessing letters of the alphabet that they think could be in the word(s).

4. If a letter in the word is guessed correctly, that letter is put in the appropriate space(s). If a letter is guessed incorrectly, a part of a snowman is drawn on the board (head, hat, arm, broom, etc.).

5. The object of the game is to guess the word or phrase before the entire snowman is drawn on the board.

Awesome Activity

Who's Santa?

Getting started: To begin the game, explain to the children that Rudolph is waiting for Santa so that all of the children's presents can be delivered. He needs to find Santa, who is hiding.

When you are ready to play: Have all of the children sit in a circle. One child is selected to be Rudolph and leaves the room while Santa is selected. One person from the circle is chosen to be Santa and then Rudolph is called back to sit in the circle. Once Rudolph returns, Santa can start winking at people in the circle. Anyone who sees that he or she has been winked at lets out a loud "HO! HO! HO!—Merry Christmas." Once Rudolph identifies who Santa is, the game begins again, with two new people being chosen to be Santa and Rudolph.

Object of the game: Rudolph needs to figure out who Santa is.

From Beth Maddigan and Stefanie Drennan, *The BIG Book of Reading, Rhyming, and Resources: Programs for Children Ages 4-8*. Westport, CT: Libraries Unlimited. © 2005.

Six to Eight Year Olds:
Week 4—Christmas Creations

Kris Kringle Candy Container

Handy Hint 1—*You will need jam or baby food jars for this craft. Send home a note for parents/caregivers at the beginning of the year, month, or unit to be sure that you have enough.*

Handy Hint 2—*Buy some red, white, and green Christmas jujubes for the children to put in their jars. It looks neat and the children will love the treat! Ask parents/caregivers before giving out food to a group of children. Children may have food allergies or sensitivities that can be dangerous.*

Materials

Jam or baby food jars—1 per child

Glue sticks

Rubber cement

Cotton balls—10 per child

Red construction paper

Small red pom-poms

Medium wiggle eyes—2 per child

Instructions

1. Photocopy (and enlarge), cut out, and trace the circle template onto red construction paper. Cut out one red circle per child.

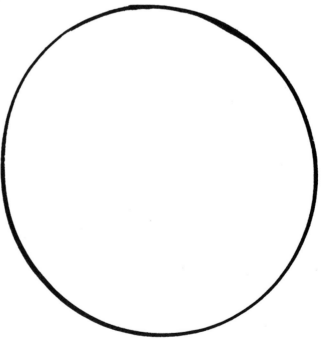

From Beth Maddigan and Stefanie Drennan, *The BIG Book of Reading, Rhyming, and Resources: Programs for Children Ages 4-8*. Westport, CT: Libraries Unlimited. © 2005.

Six to Eight Year Olds:
Week 4—Christmas Creations

2. Place a dot in the center of the circle and cut a slit from one edge of the circle to the dot.

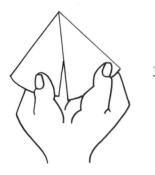

3. Overlap the edges of the slit to form a cone. Hold the cone over the baby food jar and adjust it until it just fits over the lid.

4. Using rubber cement, glue round the top rim of the lid and place the cone on top. Apply light pressure to secure the cone in place (this is Santa's hat). Because of the use of rubber cement, this step should be done ahead of time.

5. Have the children glue a cotton ball on the top and around the edges of the hat. Set aside.

6. Using a glue stick, put glue on the jar in a U shape (for the beard and hair).

7. Glue on the wiggle eyes and small red pom-pom nose.

Six to Eight Year Olds: After School Adventures

Let's Get Started!

Welcome to the third program in our chapter. With no set theme in this program, you are free to choose from any of the wonderful resources you may have at your fingertips, including the ones provided for you here. Incorporate some of your favourite games and activities and share some of your favourite books. Ask your group what their favourite games, activities, and read-alouds are. They may be a variation of some of those listed throughout this chapter.

In this program we have included some of our familiar favourites as well as some new games and activities that are sure to have your group wanting to play them over and over again! The **Books to Share** have only one theme in common: they are read-alouds that are fun to read aloud. The adventure begins now . . .

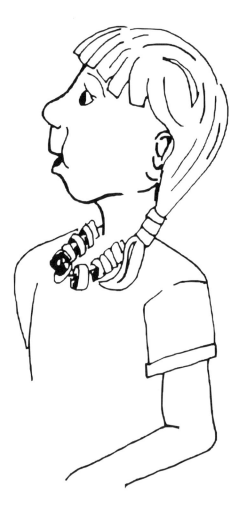

Six to Eight Year Olds: After School Adventures

The following programs contain enough stories, games, and activities to cover a one-hour session with your group. Every week should begin in the same way. A typical one-hour session would be planned and implemented in the following manner:

- **Hand out name tags**—Handing them out each week by calling the children up to get them, instead of having them on the table for the children to pick up themselves, helps you to learn the children's names more quickly.

  Time Frame—5 minutes

- **Great Games**—There are four new and different games to play with your group in this program filled with after school adventures. From "Quick Change" artistry to team trivia time, you're sure to have fun and learn some interesting facts along the way!

  Time Frame—10 minutes

- **Story**—Try to include a story that will follow up on or tie together the main theme of the program.

  Time Frame—5 minutes

- **Crafty Creation**—Show your example to give the children a brief understanding of what they will be making. Be careful not to give too many instructions (if there are quite a few) to begin with. If the craft requires a lot of explanation, do it one step at a time so the group doesn't get confused. The Craft Creation is done toward the beginning of the program to allow time for drying if needed.

  Time Frame—15 minutes

- **Awesome Activity**—This is the best opportunity to get the children moving and thinking after sitting during the beginning of the program.

  Time Frame—10 minutes

- **Story/Video**—Gather the group together and use the last few minutes to read a final story or watch a short video. Don't forget to remind the children that there are books available for borrowing or browsing.

  Time Frame—7 minutes

- **Choosing a story and dismissal**—Let the group browse through the books you have chosen to display. Once they have chosen a book (or not), they can then be dismissed.

  Time Frame—3 minutes

From Beth Maddigan and Stefanie Drennan, *The BIG Book of Reading, Rhyming, and Resources: Programs for Children Ages 4-8*. Westport, CT: Libraries Unlimited. © 2005.

Six to Eight Year Olds:
Week 1—After School Adventures

Books to Share

Bedhead by Margie Palatini

Bad Boys by Margie Palatini

Gerald McBoing Boing by Dr. Seuss

Cock-A-Doodle Moooo: A Mixed-Up Menagerie by Keith DuQuette

Great Game

Quick Change Artist

Getting started: Have everyone sit in a circle and choose one person to be the quick change artist.

When you are ready to play: Have the artist go out of sight and change something on himself or herself that is visible. (E.g., put a piece of clothing on backwards, untie one shoelace, remove one earring, etc.) When the artist is done, have him or her walk to the middle of the circle and turn around slowly to give everyone a chance to see what has been changed. Then go around the circle having each person guess what is different.

Object of the game: To figure out what the artist changed. The first person to guess correctly is the next artist.

Awesome Activity

Someone Moved

Getting started: Have all of the players sit in a circle.

When you are ready to play: Choose one player to be "it." The person chosen to be "it" must step outside of the room so that he or she cannot see or hear the remaining players in the circle. Have one to four players sitting in the circle switch places with another player.

Object of the game: When "it" returns, he or she must figure out who has moved.

From Beth Maddigan and Stefanie Drennan, *The BIG Book of Reading, Rhyming, and Resources: Programs for Children Ages 4-8*. Westport, CT: Libraries Unlimited. © 2005.

Six to Eight Year Olds:
Week 1—After School Adventures

Picture Perfect Parachutes

Handy Hint 1—Send home a note to parents and caregivers a few weeks in advance for this craft. It may take a while to collect all of the film canisters you will need.

Handy Hint 2—To add some weight, place a couple of small rocks in the container.

Materials

35mm film containers—1 per child

Plastic bags—1 per child

String

Decorating materials—stickers, permanent markers

Instructions

1. Cut a 10-by-10-inch/25-by-25 cm piece of plastic from a plastic bag.

2. Cut four pieces of string approximately 4 inches/10 cm long.

3. Tie a piece of string to each corner of the plastic square.

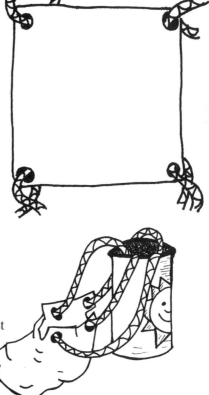

4. Put the loose ends of the string in the container, just the ends, then snap on the cap.

Six to Eight Year Olds:
Week 1—After School Adventures

5. Decorate the film canisters with stickers and the parachute with permanent markers.

6. Fold your parachute in half and then roll it down so that it touches the top of the film canister.

7. Throw it up in the air and watch it float to the ground.

Six to Eight Year Olds:
Week 2—After School Adventures

There Was an Old Woman Who Lived in a Boot by Linda Smith

Aunt Lucy Went to Buy a Hat by Alice Low

The Yawn Heard 'Round the World by Scott Thomas

The Snail and the Whale by Julia Donaldson

Great Game

Petcha Didn't Know

Getting started: Cut fifteen 4-by-5-inch/10-by-13 cm index cards in half. Using the list of questions and answers provided, write one question on each of the cards. (There are 29 questions in case you need a tie-breaker.) Make sure you put the answer on the card as well. Photocopy two each of the True and False cards (one set for each team) and back them onto cardstock to make them sturdier.

When you are ready to play: Divide your group into two teams and have them each decide on a team name. Give one person in each group a set of True and False cards. Begin by asking a question and let the group discuss the possible answers. Allow thirty seconds for discussion and then ask the person holding the cards to pick a True or False card (the one that corresponds with the answer that the team feels is the correct one) and hold it in the air. Tell the groups the answer and give a group one point for answering correctly. Continue playing until all of the questions have been asked or until you run out of time.

With each new question that you ask, have a new person holding the answer cards.

Object of the game: The group will learn some interesting new facts about animals. The team with the most points is the winner.

From Beth Maddigan and Stefanie Drennan, *The BIG Book of Reading, Rhyming, and Resources: Programs for Children Ages 4-8*. Westport, CT: Libraries Unlimited. © 2005.

Six to Eight Year Olds:
Week 2—After School Adventures

Trivia Questions

1. A cat's jaw cannot move sideways. Answer: True
2. Every spider web is the same. Answer: False
3. Dogs have ten different vocal sounds. Answer: True
4. A cow gives nearly 200,000 glasses of milk each year. Answer: True
5. Certain frogs can be frozen solid, then thawed, and continue living. Answer: True
6. Snakes are immune to their own poison. Answer: True
7. The mouse is the most common mammal in the United States. Answer: True
8. The loudest sound produced by an animal is the owl's screech. Answer: False; it's the sound of the blue whale.
9. Ants don't sleep. Answer: True
10. A mockingbird can imitate any sound it hears. Answer: True
11. All birds can fly backwards. Answer: False; hummingbirds cannot.
12. A goldfish will lose its colour if it doesn't get any sunlight. Answer: True
13. The bottom of a horse's hoof is called a frog. Answer: True
14. Two different types of penguins are named Macaroni and Emperor. Answer: True
15. A 1,200 pound horse eats ten times its own weight each year. Answer: False; it eats seven times its own weight.
16. Cats have five different vocal sounds. Answer: False; they have over 100.
17. Baby beavers are called cats. False; they are called kittens.
18. Camels have two eyelids to protect themselves from blowing sand. Answer: False; they have three eyelids.
19. A woodpecker can peck fifty times a second. Answer: False; it can peck twenty times a second.
20. Only full-grown male crickets can chirp. Answer: True
21. Some baby giraffes are more than 6 feet tall when they are born. Answer: True
22. A cat has forty muscles in each ear. Answer: False; it has thirty-two muscles in each ear.
23. A newborn kangaroo is 1 foot in length. Answer: False; it's 1 inch in length.
24. The spine-tailed swift has been clocked flying up to 220 miles per hour. Answer: True
25. An iguana can stay underwater for twenty-eight minutes. Answer: True
26. Pigs, walruses, and light-coloured horses can get sunburned. Answer: True
27. A zebra is black with white stripes. Answer: False; it's white with black stripes.
28. Large kangaroos can jump more than 100 feet with each jump. Answer: False; they can jump up to 30 feet.
29. The hummingbird, the loon, the swift, and the kingfisher are all types of birds that can walk forward and backward. Answer: False; they cannot walk at all.

From Beth Maddigan and Stefanie Drennan, *The BIG Book of Reading, Rhyming, and Resources: Programs for Children Ages 4-8*. Westport, CT: Libraries Unlimited. © 2005.

Six to Eight Year Olds:
Week 2—After School Adventures

Awesome Activity

Pick Up

Getting started: Find an object, any size, and have your group link arms and stand in a circle.

When you are ready to play: Place the object in the center of the circle and instruct your group that someone in the circle needs to pick up the object. There is one catch: the circle must remain intact. Players may use their hands, but their arms must stay linked with the player on either side of them. If the circle breaks, the game must start over. You can make this game more interesting by starting with a large object and moving to smaller and smaller objects to change the degree of difficulty. Or, make the object a bag of wrapped candies (enough for the group of course) and once they are picked up, let the group enjoy them. Ask parents/caregivers before giving out food to a group of children. Children may have food allergies or sensitivities that can be dangerous.

Object of the game: To pick up the object in the center of the circle without breaking it.

From Beth Maddigan and Stefanie Drennan, *The BIG Book of Reading, Rhyming, and Resources: Programs for Children Ages 4-8*. Westport, CT: Libraries Unlimited. © 2005.

Six to Eight Year Olds: Week 2—After School Adventures

Crafty Creation

Wonderfully Windy Wind-Up

Materials

Small margarine container lids—1 per child

Thin cereal box cardboard (1 cereal box should do 4 crafts)

Plain paper—any colour—1 sheet per child

Construction paper—any colour—1 sheet per child

Pencils

Scissors

Glue sticks—enough for your group

Push pins

Yarn

Hole punch

Instructions

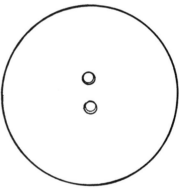

1. Trace the plastic lid once on the cardboard, once on the plain paper, and twice on the construction paper.

2. Cut out all four circles and glue one of the construction paper circles onto each side of the cardboard circles. Allow the glue to dry.

3. To find the center of the disc, take the plain paper circle and fold it in half and then in half again. Unfold it and make a mark where the two folds meet.

4. Place it on the cardboard disc and poke the push pin through the center of the circles.

Six to Eight Year Olds:
Week 2—After School Adventures

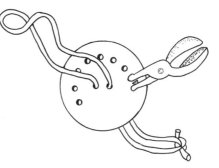

5. Make small holes (large enough for the yarn) to the right and left of the center hole.

6. Thread the yarn into the holes and knot the loose ends tightly.

7. Using the hole punch, punch a ring of holes into the disc.

8. To make the toy spin, hold a yarn loop in each hand. Slide the disc to the middle of the string and let it hang down a little. Spin the disc until the yarn on each side of it is twisted. Slowly pull your hands apart so that the disc spins quickly. When it begins to slow down, move your hands closer together to allow the toy to wind itself back up again. Keep this in and out motion going and, as it speeds up, you'll hear the wind howling.

You can decorate this toy with markers or simple construction paper shapes. Be sure not to use any craft materials that are too heavy or your disc will not spin.

From Beth Maddigan and Stefanie Drennan, *The BIG Book of Reading, Rhyming, and Resources: Programs for Children Ages 4-8*. Westport, CT: Libraries Unlimited. © 2005.

Six to Eight Year Olds:
Week 3—After School Adventures

Books to Share

Martian Rock by Carol Diggery Shields

The Magical, Mystical, Marvelous Coat by Catherine Ann Cullen

The Garbage Monster by Joni Sensel

Ed and Fred Flea by Pamela Duncan Edwards

Great Game

Believe It or Not

Getting started: Cut fourteen 4-by-5-inch/10-by-13 cm index cards in half. Using the list of questions and answers provided, write one question on each of the cards. (There are 27 questions in case you need a tie-breaker.) Make sure you put the answer on the card as well. Photocopy two each of the cards that say Believe It and Not (one set for each team) and back them onto cardstock to make them sturdier.

When you're ready to play: Divide your group into two teams and have them each decide on a team name. Give one person in each group a set of Believe It and Not cards. Begin by asking a question and let the group discuss the possible answers. Allow thirty seconds for discussion and then ask the person holding the cards to pick a Believe It or a Not card (the one that corresponds with the answer that the team feels is the correct one) and hold it in the air. Tell the groups the answer and give a group one point if they answered correctly. Continue playing until all of the questions have been asked or until you run out of time.

With each new question that you ask, have a new person holding the answer cards.

Object of the game: The group will learn some interesting new facts. The team with the most points is the winner.

Six to Eight Year Olds:
Week 3—After School Adventures

Trivia Questions

1. A hummingbirds' wings can beat 1,000 times a second. Not; they beat ninety times a second.

2. A year on Mars is the same as a year (365 days) on Earth. Not; a year on Mars is 687 days.

3. Cats can vocalize more than 100 sounds and dogs can only vocalize 10. Believe It

4. A person is most likely to see a UFO between 9:00 and 10:00 P.M. during the month of January. Believe It

5. Cats spend an average of ten hours a day sleeping. Not; they actually spend approximately sixteen hours a day sleeping.

6. In the book *Alice in Wonderland,* the Mad Hatter was "late for a very important date." Not; it was the White Rabbit

7. Lions are the biggest cats in the world. Not; tigers are the biggest cats in the world.

8. No species of bear can swim. Not; all bears can swim and love the water.

9. In the book *Pinocchio,* when Pinocchio lied he grew a tail. Not; his nose grew.

10. In the book *Cinderella,* Cinderella had five wonderful stepsisters. Not; she had two mean stepsisters.

11. Bats are the only mammals that can fly. Believe It; their wings are really webbed hands.

12. The koala bear and the cat are considered two of the ten laziest creatures in the world. Believe It.

13. In 1990, over 10,000 UFO sightings were reported from all over the world. Believe It.

14. You can tell how a horse is feeling by looking at its body. Believe It; if its ears are laid back, it is ready to fight. If it is pawing at the ground with its front hoof, it is impatient.

15. A human heart beats one million times a day. Not; a human heart beats 100,000 times a day.

16. Pluto is the largest planet in the solar system. Not; the largest planet is Jupiter.

17. A herbivore is an animal that eats plants and other animals. Not; a herbivore only eats plants.

18. You can tell the age of a horse by looking at its teeth. Believe It.

19. Dinosaurs are believed to be on Earth for over 400 million years. Not; they are believed to have been here for 165 million years.

20. There are over 500 bones in the human body. Not; there are 206.

21. Saltwater crocodiles in Northern Australia grow to be up to 50 feet long. Not; the average length is 20 feet.

22. A great white shark has five rows of teeth in its mouth. Not; a great white shark has three rows of teeth.

23. Sea otters sleep in the water by lying on their backs and wrapping themselves in seaweed so they don't get swept away by the current. Believe It.

24. The largest library in the world is in Washington, D.C. It contains 29 million books. Believe It.

25. A dog's most highly developed sense is its sight. Not.; a dog's most highly developed sense is smell.

26. UFO stands for Unidentified Flying Object. Believe It.

27. The word *dinosaur* actually means "scaly hunter." Not; it actually means "terrible lizard."

From Beth Maddigan and Stefanie Drennan, *The BIG Book of Reading, Rhyming, and Resources: Programs for Children Ages 4-8*. Westport, CT: Libraries Unlimited. © 2005.

Six to Eight Year Olds:
Week 3—After School Adventures

Awesome Activity

I Sailed a Ship from A to Z

Getting started: Have your group sit in a circle.

When you're ready to play: The leader should start this game. The leader begins by saying the following phrase:

> I sailed a ship across the sea,
>
> And on the way home I brought with me _____

Fill in the blank with something that begins with the letter A (e.g., apples). The next person in the circle would say:

> I sailed a ship across the sea,
>
> And on the way home I brought with me <u>apples and bananas</u> *(or something beginning with B)*

Play continues this way (the next person is C and then D) with each person naming what each other player brought. Always start with A and continue on until they reach the next letter in the alphabet.

Object of the game: To see how far the group can make it around the circle with everyone remembering what object each other player named.

From Beth Maddigan and Stefanie Drennan, *The BIG Book of Reading, Rhyming, and Resources: Programs for Children Ages 4-8*. Westport, CT: Libraries Unlimited. © 2005.

Six to Eight Year Olds:
Week 3—After School Adventures

Crafty Creation

Wandering Wizards

Materials

Cardstock—1 sheet per child

Resealable storage bags—1 per child

Scissors

Glue sticks

Decorating materials—pencil crayons, markers

Instructions

1. Photocopy two copies of the Wandering Wizards puzzle per child and cut along the outer box edge, keeping the large square intact. The second copy can be used as an answer key if anyone has trouble putting the puzzle together again at home.

2. Back one puzzle onto cardstock and colour it.

3. Cut the coloured puzzle into twenty squares, being careful to follow the lines.

4. Have the children try to put their puzzles together again without looking at the answer sheet. Good Luck!

From Beth Maddigan and Stefanie Drennan, *The BIG Book of Reading, Rhyming, and Resources: Programs for Children Ages 4-8*. Westport, CT: Libraries Unlimited. © 2005.

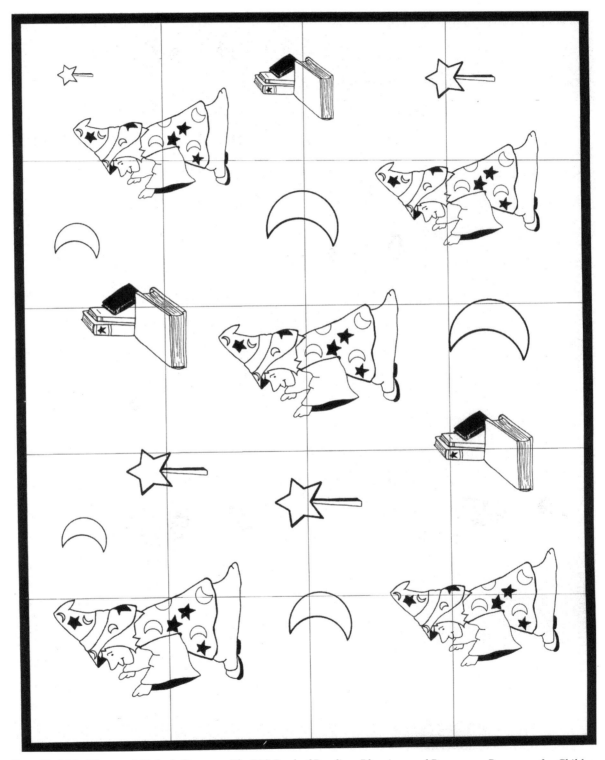

Six to Eight Year Olds:
Week 4—After School Adventures

Very Boring Alligator by Jean Gralley

Alberto the Dancing Dinosaur by Richard Waring

Naughty Little Monkeys by Jim Aylesworth

Bugs! by Pat McKissack

Great Game

Operation "Obstacle"

Getting started: Choose either to divide the group into two teams or have the entire group play together. Have them form two lines, one behind the other, or have the group play as a whole. The first person in the line is the leader for this game

When you are ready to play: Each player must choose whether he or she is an "under," "left," or "right" obstacle. At the signal (count down from 3, blow a whistle) the leader proceeds down the line as told by each obstacle. If a player says left or right, the leader must go left or right around that player; if a player says under, the leader must go under that player's legs. Each player, after the leader passes, then follows. When the leader reaches the end, he or she then becomes an obstacle, and play continues until all have passed him or her and the line is as it was in the beginning.

Object of the game: A great game for the group to play as a whole or, if you choose to have two separate teams, the winning team is the team to get their line back to its original order first.

Awesome Activity

Stormy Weather

Getting started: Have your group sit in a circle.

When you are ready to play: Instruct the group to close their eyes before you begin. Select a leader. The leader starts this game by rubbing his or her palms together. The person to the right of the leader follows, and so on until the person to the left of the leader has started. Then the leader snaps his or her fingers or begins drumming his or her hands on the floor. This continues around the circle until it also reaches the leader. Then the leader starts clapping and this proceeds around, then slapping thighs, then stomping feet. By now the storm is fully under way, and at this time the leader reverses the slapping, clapping, drumming, snapping, and rubbing of hands until all is quiet and the rain has passed.

Object of the game: A great group activity that gets better and better with practice.

From Beth Maddigan and Stefanie Drennan, *The BIG Book of Reading, Rhyming, and Resources: Programs for Children Ages 4-8*. Westport, CT: Libraries Unlimited. © 2005.

Six to Eight Year Olds:
Week 4—After School Adventure

Crafty Creation

Realistic Rainsticks

Materials

Paper towel tubes—1 per person

Aluminium (tin) foil

Small dried beans, lentils, unpopped popcorn, or dry rice—1 handful per person

Brown construction paper—1 sheet per person

Construction paper—various colors—1 per child

Glue sticks

Scissors

Decorating materials—markers, stickers, foam pieces

Instructions

1. Trace around the end of the paper towel roll twice onto the brown construction paper. Draw a larger circle around the traced circle and then draw spokes between the two circles (see illustration).

2. Cut out the circles and then cut along the spokes.

3. Put glue on the spokes and glue one cap onto one end of your tube.

4. Cut a piece of aluminium foil that is 1½ times the length of your tube and 6 inches/15 cm wide. Cut this in half vertically so that you have two long pieces of aluminium foil to work with.

From Beth Maddigan and Stefanie Drennan, *The BIG Book of Reading, Rhyming, and Resources: Programs for Children Ages 4-8*. Westport, CT: Libraries Unlimited. © 2005.

Six to Eight Year Olds:
Week 4—After School Adventure

5. Crunch the aluminium foil into two long, thin, snakelike shapes. Twist each of these into a spring (coil) shape.

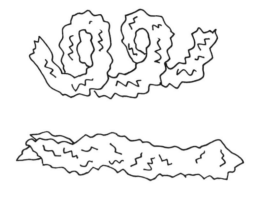

6. Put the aluminium foil springs (coils) into your tube.

7. Pour some dry beans, rice, or unpopped popcorn into the tube. The tube should only be about 10 percent full. You can experiment to see how different amounts and different types of seeds change the sound.

8. Glue the second cap onto the open end of the tube.

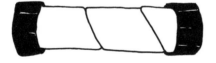

9. Decorate the tube by wrapping a piece of coloured construction paper around it and taping it in place. Children can then decorate the tube with markers, stickers, or foam pieces.

From Beth Maddigan and Stefanie Drennan, *The BIG Book of Reading, Rhyming, and Resources: Programs for Children Ages 4-8*. Westport, CT: Libraries Unlimited. © 2005.

Six to Eight Year Olds: Fun and Games

Let's Get Started!

Here we are at the final program in this chapter, and it's been so much fun, we thought we would name it just that: Fun and Games. The following four weeks also take a less structured approach to programming and have no set theme to work with. The **Books to Share** have been chosen based on the fact that they are hilarious and great to read aloud to this age group. The games and activities are a nice break from the traditional but can still be adapted to fit into a theme-based program, and the **Crafty Creations** are simple and require little prep time. Have fun!

Six to Eight Year Olds: Fun and Games

The following programs contain enough stories, games, and activities to cover a one-hour session with your group. Every week should begin in the same way. A typical one-hour session would be planned and implemented in the following manner:

- **Hand out name tags**—Handing them out each week by calling the children up to get them, instead of having them on the table for the children to pick up themselves, helps you to learn the children's names more quickly.

  Time Frame—5 minutes

- *Great Games*—There are four new and different games to play with your group in this program filled with fun and games. From "Questionable Quizzing" to "Grand Giggling," you're sure to have fun and learn some interesting facts along the way!

  Time Frame—10 minutes

- **Story**—Try to include a story that will follow up on or tie together the main theme of the program.

  Time Frame—5 minutes

- **Crafty Creation**—Show your example to give the children a brief understanding of what they will be making. Be careful not to give too many instructions (if there are quite a few) to begin with. If the craft requires a lot of explanation, do it one step at a time so the group doesn't get confused. The Crafty Creation is done toward the beginning of the program to allow time for drying if needed.

  Time Frame—15 minutes

- **Awesome Activity**—This is the best opportunity to get the children moving and thinking after sitting during the beginning of the program.

  Time Frame—10 minutes

- **Story/Video**—Gather the group together and use the last few minutes to read a final story or watch a short video. Don't forget to remind the children that there are books available for borrowing or browsing.

  Time Frame—7 minutes

- **Choosing a story and dismissal**—Let the group browse through the books you have chosen to display. Once they have chosen a book (or not), they can then be dismissed.

  Time Frame—3 minutes

From Beth Maddigan and Stefanie Drennan, *The BIG Book of Reading, Rhyming, and Resources: Programs for Children Ages 4-8*. Westport, CT: Libraries Unlimited. © 2005.

Six to Eight Year Olds:
Week 1—Fun and Games

Books to Share

My Little Sister Ate One Hare by Bill Grossman

Slithery Jake by Rose Marie Burns

Here Come the Blobbies by Jorge

Saturday Night at the Dinosaur Stomp by Carol Diggery Shields

Great Game

Grand Giggler

Getting started: Have your group sit in a circle.

When you are ready to play: Choose one person to be the Grand Giggler. The Grand Giggler will smile a big smile at all of the players, trying to get them to crack a smile or laugh. Anyone who does smile or laugh is out and must wait for the next round to join back in. The Grand Giggler can wipe the smile off of his or her face and toss it to another player if he or she wishes. The receiving player will put on the smile and be the new Grand Giggler.

Object of the game: All players try to keep a straight face while the Grand Giggler tries to eliminate them one by one by making them smile.

You may wish to put a time limit on each Grand Giggler or make it a Giggler challenge. See who can make the most people smile or laugh in a certain amount of time.

Awesome Activity

Tasty Treat Trivia

A game that's so much fun your group will want to play it every day! Ask parents/caregivers before giving out food to a group of children. Children may have food allergies or sensitivities that can be dangerous.

Getting started: Purchase a few bags of coloured candies such as M&Ms or Skittles. Make sure you have enough so that every player in your group can have three or four.

From Beth Maddigan and Stefanie Drennan, *The BIG Book of Reading, Rhyming, and Resources: Programs for Children Ages 4-8*. Westport, CT: Libraries Unlimited. © 2005.

Six to Eight Year Olds:
Week 1—Fun and Games

When you are ready to play: Pass the candies around the room and have each person take three or four different coloured candies and place them in front of him or her. After the whole group has them, explain that they need to stand, say their names, and tell the following things based on the colour of candy that they selected.

Colour Code:

Dark brown—favourite TV show

Light brown—favourite movie

Yellow—favourite sport

Red—favourite outdoor activity

Blue—favourite vacation

Green—favourite fast food restaurant

Orange—favourite band/type of music

Purple—favourite colour

Object of the game: A tasty way to learn more about fellow group members or classmates.

From Beth Maddigan and Stefanie Drennan, *The BIG Book of Reading, Rhyming, and Resources: Programs for Children Ages 4-8*. Westport, CT: Libraries Unlimited. © 2005.

Six to Eight Year Olds: Week 1—Fun and Games

Crafty Creation

Fantastic Flying Frisbees™!

Materials

Paper plates—4 per child—any size

Glue sticks

Decorating materials—paint, stickers, markers

Instructions

1. Cut out the centers from four paper plates.

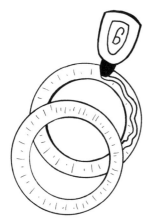

2. Decorate two of the rings using paints, stickers, markers, or other decorating materials.

3. Glue the four rings together so that the decorated rings are top and bottom.

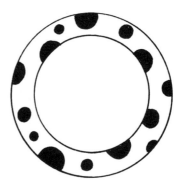

Six to Eight Year Olds:
Week 1—Fun and Games

To make the Frisbee fly:

1. Hold the Frisbee about chest height. Bend your hand towards your body.

2. With a flick of your wrist, release the Frisbee. It should travel parallel to the ground, not up into the air.

Six to Eight Year Olds:
Week 2—Fun and Games

Books to Share

The Rules by Marty Kelley

What Are You So Grumpy About? by Tom Lichtenhold

Bubble Trouble by Joy N. Hulme

The Fish Who Could Wish by John Bush

Great Game

Tricky Answer Trivia

Getting started: Gather your group together and have them sit in a circle.

When you are ready to play: Begin this game by having the programmer be the leader. Later as the group becomes more comfortable with how to play, a child can try out the role of leader. Begin by asking one person at a time a question. He or she must answer the question *incorrectly*. Each person should respond within one or two seconds to keep this game moving at a fast pace. Players can be out of the game if they do one of the following three things:

1. Take too long to answer.

2. Stumble as they answer.

3. Give the correct answer.

As the programmer, you decide whether you want children to be out or whether you simply want to see how many children you can trick into giving the correct answers.

Object of the game: To keep a continuous cycle of questions and answers going around the circle.

Six to Eight Year Olds: Week 2—Fun and Games

Tricky Trivia Questions

1. What day comes after Friday?
2. How many hands do you have?
3. How old are you?
4. What is your name?
5. What city do you live in?
6. What country do you live in?
7. Are you bald?
8. What letter comes after Y?
9. What year is this?
10. What is 2 + 2?
11. What number comes after 2?
12. What month is this?
13. What day is this?
14. What street do you live on?
15. What are you sitting on?
16. Are you wearing shoes?
17. What colour is the sky?
18. How many fingers do you have?
19. What school do you go to?
20. How many fingers am I holding up? (Leader holds up fingers.)
21. Finish this song title: "Twinkle, Twinkle Little _____."

Awesome Activity

Two Truths and a Lie

Getting started: Have everyone come up with two things about themselves that are true and one that is not and write them down on a piece of paper. Instruct the group not to show anyone else what they have written.

When you're ready to play: Gather your group into a circle and choose one person to begin the game. That person should stand and read what he or she has written out loud to the group, who then must decide which of the three things are true and which one is a lie.

Example: The three things I could say about myself are: I've been to Mexico, I have two cats, and I am allergic to flowers.

When everyone has made a choice of which one they think is not true, the person can then reveal the two truths and the lie.

Object of the game: A great way to get to know your group while keeping everyone involved.

From Beth Maddigan and Stefanie Drennan, *The BIG Book of Reading, Rhyming, and Resources: Programs for Children Ages 4-8*. Westport, CT: Libraries Unlimited. © 2005.

Six to Eight Year Olds:
Week 2—Fun and Games

Crafty Creation

Scoop Ball

Handy Hint—*Send home a note with your group a couple of weeks in advance asking parents to send in a laundry detergent scoop with their children (more than one if possible).*

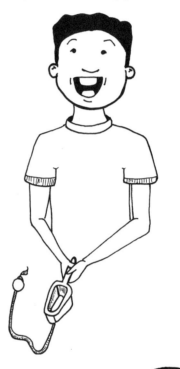

Materials

Laundry scoops—large or small—2 per child

Yarn or string

Large beads

Masking tape

Decorating materials—stickers, glitter, glue

Instructions

1. Cut a length of string approximately 12 inches/30 cm in length.

2. Tie one end of the string securely to a bead by looping it through the hole and tying a knot.

3. Tape the other end of the string to the bottom of the outside of the scoop.

4. Decorate the scoop or leave it as is.

5. Try to catch the bead in the scoop.

From Beth Maddigan and Stefanie Drennan, *The BIG Book of Reading, Rhyming, and Resources: Programs for Children Ages 4-8.* Westport, CT: Libraries Unlimited. © 2005.

Six to Eight Year Olds: Week 3—Fun and Games

The Stinky Cheese Man; and Other Fairly Stupid Tales by Jon Scieszka

Timothy Tunny Swallowed A Bunny by Bill Grossman

Skunks by David T. Greenburg

Gilbert De La Frogponde: A Swamp Story by Jennifer Ral

Great Game

Questionable Quizzing

Getting started: Have your group gathered and sitting in a circle.

When you're ready to play: Decide whether you will start the questions moving clockwise or counterclockwise around the circle. The first player faces the player to his or her right and asks a question. There is no minimum or maximum length for the questions, and the player does not answer the question he or she is asked. Instead, he or she turns to the player on his or her right and asks that person a question. The next player asks the player to his or her right a question, and so on. Players should look at the person who is asking them the question and then at the player of whom they are asking the question.

A player is out or the chain breaks (causing you to stop and start at the player who broke the chain) when he or she

1. answers the question that is asked,

2. does not immediately ask the next person a question,

3. laughs,

4. makes a statement instead of asking a question, or

5. repeats a question that was very recently asked.

Object of the game: To try to get around the circle without anyone breaking the cycle of questions.

From Beth Maddigan and Stefanie Drennan, *The BIG Book of Reading, Rhyming, and Resources: Programs for Children Ages 4-8*. Westport, CT: Libraries Unlimited. © 2005.

Six to Eight Year Olds:
Week 3—Fun and Games

A What?

Getting started: Have an object on hand to use as the "what," such as a ball, a paper clip, chalk, or a brush. Anything will work.

When you are ready to play: Have your group come together and sit in a circle. The programmer should sit somewhere in the circle as well, holding the object that will be used in the game. The leader starts the game by passing the object to the person on the right and saying "This is a banana." The receiver says, "A what?" and the giver repeats, "A banana." Then the object is passed on to the third person the same way. When asked, "A what?" each person inquires of the one who gave it to him or her, "A What?" before passing it on to the next person. A typical game would start like this:

Player A—passes the object to Player B and says, "This is a banana."

Player B—says to Player A, "A What?"

Player A—says to Player B, "A banana."

Player B—passes the object to Player C and says, "This is a banana."

Player C—looks at Player B and says, "A What?"

Player B—looks at Player A and says, " A What?"

Player A—says to Player B, "A banana."

Player B—says to Player C, "A banana."

Player C—passes the object to Player D and says, "This is a banana."

Player D—says to Player C, "A What?"

Player C—looks at Player B and says, "A What?"

Player B—looks at Player A and says, "A What?"

Player A—says to Player B, "A banana."

And so on as it continues around the circle.

From Beth Maddigan and Stefanie Drennan, *The BIG Book of Reading, Rhyming, and Resources: Programs for Children Ages 4-8*. Westport, CT: Libraries Unlimited. © 2005.

Six to Eight Year Olds:
Week 3—Fun and Games

Marble Maze

Materials

Cardstock—1 sheet per person

Construction paper—various colours—1 sheet per person

Glue sticks

Popsicle sticks—10 per person

Plasticene—2 packages

Marbles—1 per person

Decorating materials—stickers, crayons, markers

Masking or transparent tape

Instructions

1. Glue a sheet of construction paper to a sheet of cardstock

2. Cut a 1-inch/2.5 cm slit, into each of the sides, near the corners (see illustration).

Six to Eight Year Olds:
Week 3—Fun and Games

3. Fold each side of the paper up to make a crease (the sides should stand up) and tape them securely into place. These are the sides to the marble maze that will prevent the marble from rolling out.

4. Provide each child with 10 Popsicle sticks (they may use fewer) and a chunk of plasticene.

5. The children can make their own marble maze by making the Popsicle sticks stand on their edges. To do this put a glob of plasticene on each end of the Popsicle stick and squish it on the paper (see illustration).

6. Decorate with stickers, markers, or crayons if desired.

7. Drop in the marble and be a-mazed!

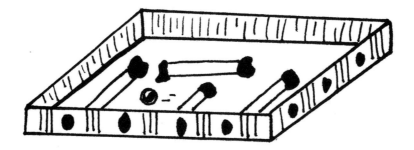

From Beth Maddigan and Stefanie Drennan, *The BIG Book of Reading, Rhyming, and Resources: Programs for Children Ages 4-8*. Westport, CT: Libraries Unlimited. © 2005.

Six to Eight Year Olds:
Week 4—Fun and Games

Books to Share

Do Pirates Take Baths? by Kathy Tucker

Incredible Ned; You Could See What He Said by Bill Maynard

Maxwell's Magic Mix-Up by Linda Ashman

Stanley's Party by Linda Bailey

Great Game

Pirate!

Handy Hint—Purchase gold coin look-alikes at your local party supply store or use the template from the Tic Tac Tub game and photocopy them onto goldenrod construction paper.

Getting started: Have your group gather together and sit in a circle.

When you are ready to play: Choose one player to be the pirate. That player will be required to sit in the middle of the circle, blindfolded (eyes closed tight is an option for anyone who gets scared) with his or her legs crossed. Place three coins in front of the pirate. Choose one player to slowly creep up, attempt to take a coin, and return to his or her place without the pirate hearing. If the pirate does hear someone trying to take his or her booty, he or she says aloud, "Ahoy Matey! Walk the plank!" and the person must return to his or her spot in the circle. The programmer will then choose another child to try again.

Object of the game: The pirate has three chances to point to where he or she thinks the thief is. If the pirate succeeds, he or she gets to choose the new pirate.

This game can also be played using sets of keys. It adds a more difficult element to the game as the jingle of the keys will be a giveaway that someone is trying to steal them.

Awesome Activity

Simon Says Switch!

Getting started: Have your group form two lines of equal numbers. The programmer should be Simon unless you have an uneven number of children in your group. In this case, one child at a time could take a turn being Simon.

When you are ready to play: As in *Simon Says,* players must obey instructions preceded by the phrase "Simon Says" but not those given without it. Anyone who goofs must switch teams.

Object of the game: To be the team with the most players when the game is over.

A variation of this game could be to have two Simons, one in each line, giving instructions and trying to trip up the players in the other line in an effort to steal team members.

From Beth Maddigan and Stefanie Drennan, *The BIG Book of Reading, Rhyming, and Resources: Programs for Children Ages 4-8.* Westport, CT: Libraries Unlimited. © 2005.

Six to Eight Year Olds: Week 4—Fun and Games

Rub-a-Dub-Dub Its . . . Tic Tac Tub!

Materials

Fun foam—red, yellow, and black—1 sheet of each colour per child

Resealable plastic bags—1 per child

Scissors

Instructions

1. Photocopy and back onto cardstock the pirate X (enlarged) and gold coin O templates and cut them out. These will be your tracers.

2. Trace the pirate X five times onto the red fun foam and cut it out.

3. Trace the gold coin onto the yellow fun foam four times and cut it out.

4. Cut four strips out of the black fun foam, 4 inches long by .4 inch wide (10 cm long by 1 cm wide).

From Beth Maddigan and Stefanie Drennan, *The BIG Book of Reading, Rhyming, and Resources: Programs for Children Ages 4-8*. Westport, CT: Libraries Unlimited. © 2005.

5. Have children match up with a partner and practice playing together. Once they are done, have them place their pieces into the sealable bags to take home. These pieces can be played with in the tub as they will stick to the sides of the bathtub once they are wet.

From Beth Maddigan and Stefanie Drennan, *The BIG Book of Reading, Rhyming, and Resources: Programs for Children Ages 4-8*. Westport, CT: Libraries Unlimited. © 2005.

Bibliography of Books to Share

Ashman, Linda. 2001. *Maxwell's Magic Mix-Up.* New York: Simon & Schuster Children's Publishing.

Aylesworth, Jim. 2003. *Naughty Little Monkeys.* New York: Dutton Books.

Bailey, Linda. 2003. *Stanley's Party.* New York: Kids Can Press.

Barry, Robert. 2000. *Mr. Willowby's Christmas Tree.* New York: Doubleday Books for Young Readers.

Brett, Jan. 1998. *The Night Before Christmas.* New York: Putnam Publishing Group.

Buehner, Caralyn. 2002. *Snowmen at Night.* New York: Dial Books.

Bunting, Eve. 1986. *Scary, Scary, Halloween.* New York: Clarion Books.

Burns, Rose Marie. 2004. *Slithery Jake.* New York. HarperCollins.

Bush, John. 1994. *The Fish Who Could Wish.* La Jolla, CA: Kane/Miller Publishers.

Christie, Michael. 2000. *Olive, the Orphan Reindeer.* New Canaan, CT: New Canaan Publishing Company.

Cullen, Catherine Ann. 2001. *The Magical, Mystical, Marvelous Coat.* New York: Little, Brown.

David, Lawrence. 2001. *Peter Claus and the Naughty List.* New York: Doubleday Books for Young Readers.

Donaldson, Julia. 2001. *Room on the Broom.* New York. Dial Books for Young Readers.

Donaldson, Julia. 2004. *The Snail and the Whale.* New York: Dial Books for Young Readers.

Edwards, Pamela Duncan. 1999. *Ed and Fred Flea.* New York. Hyperion Books for Children.

Garland, Michael. 2001. *Mystery Mansion: A Look Again Book.* New York: Dutton Books.

Garland, Michael. 1997. *The Mouse Before Christmas.* New York: Dutton Books.

Gralley, Jean. 2001. *Very Boring Alligator.* New York: Henry Holt.

Greenburg, David T. 2002. *Skunks!* New York: Little, Brown.

Grossman, Bill. 1988. *My Little Sister Ate One Hare.* Cleveland, OH: Dragonfly Books.

Grossman, Bill. 2003. *Timothy Tunny Swallowed a Bunny.* New York: HarperTrophy.

Hintz, Martin, and Kate Hintz. 1996. *Hallowe'en: Why We Celebrate It the Way We Do.* Mankato, MN: Capstone Press.

Howitt, Mary. 2002. *The Spider and the Fly.* New York: Simon & Schuster Children's Publishing.

Huck, Charlotte. 1998. *A Creepy Countdown.* New York: Greenwillow.

Hulme, Joy N. 1999. *Bubble Trouble.* San Francisco: Children's Press.

Jorge. 2003. *Here Come the Blobbies.* Santa Clara, CA: Pers Publishing.

Kelley, Marty. 2000. *The Rules.* Madison, WI: Zino Press Children's Books.

Lankford, Mary D. 1998. *Christmas Around the World.* New York: HarperTrophy.

Lesynski, Loris. 1998. *Catmagic*. Toronto: Annick Press.

Lichtenhold, Tom. 2003. *What Are You So Grumpy About?* New York: Little, Brown.

Low, Alice. 2004. *Aunt Lucy Went to Buy a Hat*. New York: HarperCollins.

Maynard, Bill. 1999. *Incredible Ned: You Could See What He Said*. New York: Putnam Publishing Group.

McKissack, Pat. 2000. *Bugs!* San Francisco: Children's Press.

Melmed, Laura Krauss. 2002. *Fright Night Flight*. New York: HarperCollins.

Osborn, Susan T. 1996. *Children Around the World Celebrate Christmas*. Cincinnati, OH: Standard Publishing Company.

Rader, Laura. 2003. *Who'll Pull Santa's Sleigh Tonight*. New York: HarperCollins.

Ral, Jennifer. 1997. *Gilbert De La Frogponde*: A Swamp Story. Atlanta, GA: Peachtree Publishers.

Reiss, Mike. 2002. *Santa Claustrophobia*. New York: Price Stern Sloan.

Sarnoff, Jane. 1980. *If You Were Really Superstitious*. New York: Scribner Book Company.

Scieszka, Jon. 2002. *The Stinky Cheese Man; And Other Fairly Stupid Tales*. New York: Viking Juvenile.

Shields, Carol Diggery. 1999. *Martian Rock*. Cambridge, MA: Candlewick Press.

Shields, Carol Diggery. 2002. *Saturday Night at the Dinosaur Stomp*. Cambridge, MA: Candlewick Press.

Sierra, Judy. 1998. *The House That Drac Built*. San Diego: Voyager Books.

Smith, Linda. 2004. *There Was an Old Woman Who Lived in a Boot*. New York: HarperCollins.

Stutson, Caroline. 1993. *By the Light of the Halloween Moon*. New York: HarperCollins.

Thomas, Scott. 2003. *The Yawn Heard 'Round the World*. New York, NY:: Tricycle Press.

Thompson, Richard. 2003. *The Follower*. Markham, ON: Fitzhenry & Whiteside Ltd.

Tucker, Kathy. 1997. *Do Pirates Take Baths?* Morton Grove, IL.: Albert Whitman.

Waring, Richard. 2002. *Alberto: The Dancing Dinosaur*. Cambridge, MA: Candlewick Press.

Wong, Janet S. 2003. *Knock on Wood: Poems About Superstitions*. New York: Margaret McElderry.

Chapter 6

Marketing and Publicity

Exciting, well-planned programs for children will ensure that attendees have a valuable experience and many of your institution's programming goals will be met. However, if attendance is low and the programs are not utilized to their fullest extent, their potential for the institution is not being realized. To be successful, to maintain that success, and to expose *new* people to the benefits of literature-based programming, it is important to market your services to the community. Some libraries find marketing and publicity is not crucial to the success of their programs. In these facilities, members learn about the programs, attend them, and tell their friends about them. This word-of-mouth advertising is enough to fill future sessions. While this approach is gratifying when it works, for many centers it is not enough. If you rely solely on in-house marketing, you may miss the potential clientele who have no idea what your institution has to offer them. For some members of the community the library, literacy center, or neighbourhood school is an intimidating institution. Adult members of your community, especially those who are not literate or those who found formal schooling difficult, will be less enthusiastic about a trip to the library or an after school program for their children at school. For other members of the community, the library, or any educational facility, is not a priority. Although they do read, they get their reading materials from other sources: bookstores, newsstands, friends, or the Internet. For whatever reason, a percentage of every community's population does not use the library. Therefore, it is important to market your facility's programs to the entire community even if you run successful programs through word-of-mouth advertising. It is important that you give those members of your community who do not see literacy as a priority a chance to expose their children to new resources, learning opportunities, and exciting literature-based programs.

1. Promoting Programs in Your Community

Public relations and marketing can be as simple or as elaborate as you make them. Some library systems have marketing departments; others do no marketing or publicity at all. If you are planning a marketing campaign, there are a number of key questions you should answer before you begin:

- Whom are you trying to reach?

- How will your programs benefit these people?

- How can you best get your message across?

- What are the key selling points of your programs?

- What obstacles stand in the way of newcomers attending your programs?

- How can you eliminate these obstacles?

The answers to these questions will give you starting points and things to think about while you decide the best way to get the word out about your programs to the community. The answers will also give you a focus for your marketing campaign, because the best marketing is specific. Marketing that focuses on a single element, audience, and program will often be the most successful. Identify whom you need to reach, reach them, and let them know how their lives will be enriched by attending your programs. If they have issues that keep them from attending, show them how these issues can be eliminated or diminished.

2. Publicity

Publicity is used to create interest or attention. Publicity methods and approaches are varied and innovative, but because most libraries and children's facilities are interested in *affordable* publicity, we discuss a few tried and true (and virtually free) methods here.

2.1 Press Releases

Media organizations such as local newspapers, magazines, and television and radio stations will accept faxed or e-mailed messages that detail an event. Figure 6.1 is an example of a simple press release. The format of the page is not as important as the message itself. To be effective the press release should be short and to the point. Be sure to include basic information about the event, but don't get bogged down in detail. Basic information usually includes "who, what, when, and where." Prominently display a contact name and number so the media outlet can call for more information. A press release should be detailed enough to give the media a story for air or print if they choose to run it without further information, but it shouldn't include every detail. Media organizations receive many of these each day, so you also need to make yours memorable. Journalists and broadcast staff deal in jazzy, unforgettable marketing daily, so they will not be fooled by glitz or graphics. Instead, highlight important elements that will appeal to the media's audience and make the event newsworthy. Convey your own excitement about the event. Be sure to send a press release for any program or event that is *new* to your facility, but do not send out releases for regularly scheduled programs. If you send too many press releases, media organizations will quickly learn to ignore everything you send.

Press Release from the Cambridge Libraries

*If you require more information about the "Magical Monstrous March Break 2004" programs offered at the Cambridge Libraries, please contact Beth Maddigan at **(519) 621-0460**.*

Magical Monstrous March Break 2004

Cast a spell this March Break at the Cambridge Libraries. All library locations will be offering a variety of monstrously magical programs for children. Make a magical dragon puppet or design your own wizard gear. Disguise yourself in a creative monster mask or use the magic powers of a crown and wand. Don't miss out, be sure to pick up your free tickets for these and other exciting programs at the library.

Enjoy a juggling extravaganza and interactive show with "The Silly People." And don't miss Dr. Kidd's amazing and interactive magic show. Minimal fees will be charged for entertainers.

Experience all of these programs and much, much more March 10 through March 17. There are programs open to children of all ages. Parental supervision may be required for some programs.

For more information about this magical extravaganza, drop by your nearest library location or call 621-0460 and ask for Children's Services.

Figure 6.1. Press Release from the Cambridge Libraries

2.2 Public Service Announcements

If you are providing literature-based children's programs to members of the community for little or no cost, your institution is providing a public service. Call local media and ask if they air or print public service announcements. If they do, find out what their specifications are. Often there are length requirements, and some agencies will only announce events for charitable or nonprofit organizations. Figure 6.2 is a public service announcement for an after school program offered by the library. The key to public service announcements is to keep them short but readable. Radio and television stations like announcements that they can read directly from the page, so review your public service announcement and read it aloud several times to work on the way it *sounds*, not the way it looks. Try to keep your announcement to ten seconds or less when read aloud at a reasonable pace. This seems like very little time, but in fact all you need to do is catch people's attention, and a short, specific announcement does this best. Some radio and TV stations will run thirty-second announcements, but you have a better chance of having your announcement read on the air if it reads in ten seconds.

Public Service Announcement from the Cambridge Libraries.

Please read or print the information that follows about an exciting new program offered by the Cambridge Libraries with any community advertising you provide.

For more information, please contact Beth Maddigan, Children's Services Coordinator, at 621-0460.

Calling all six to eight year olds. Join us at the library on Wednesdays in November for an after school adventure. The program is free, but space is limited. Call 621-0460 for more information.

Figure 6.2. Public Service Announcement from the Cambridge Libraries

2.3 Flyers

Publish a one-page flyer to announce your program and photocopy it onto bright-coloured paper. Ask local businesses, organizations, churches, and community groups to post it. Businesses and agencies foster relationships with reputable organizations, so they will often welcome a flyer for a free program at the local library. Target businesses that have a tie-in for your program. Running a preschool program? Contact businesses that sell products for preschoolers. Starting a new family program? Contact agencies that deal with families in your community, including retailers and social service agencies. Use graphics and text in ways that enhance your message, not confuse it. Be sure flyers are eye-catching but simple. Leave a significant amount of white space around elements you want to focus on. Don't try to include every detail someone might want to know about your organization. Instead, simply show people what you are doing and why they would want to come. Don't forget to feature the location and your facility's name prominently. If you can get prior permission, flyers can also be put on the windshields of cars at the local mall. Or they can be distributed, usually relatively inexpensively, with the local paper. Figure 6.3 is a sample of a flyer that was used to promote the library's children's program registration.

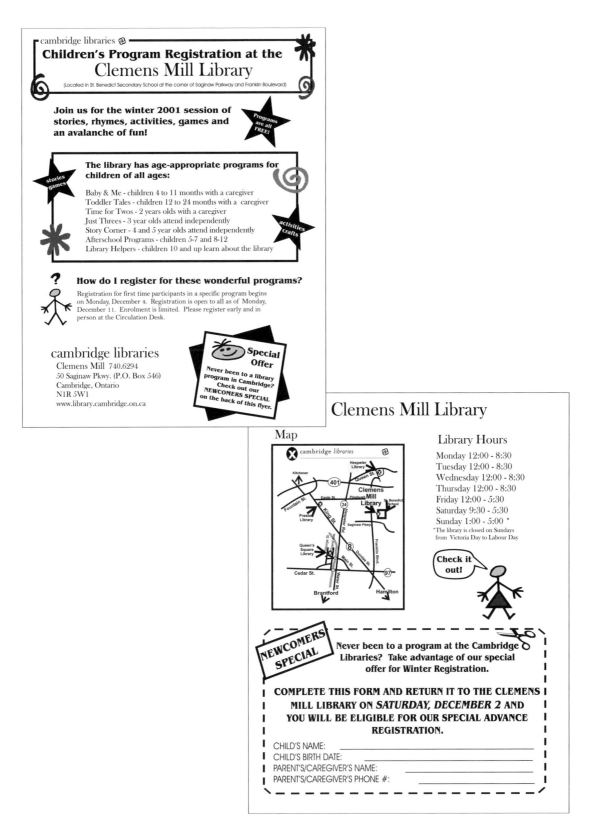

Figure 6.3. Library Children's Promotion (Two-Page Spread)

To use any of these elements effectively, you need to do a little legwork. Get to know your community and its agencies, businesses, and local media. Make follow-up calls when you send an announcement. By establishing relationships with agencies that may reach a clientele your library does not reach, you are increasing your programming potential and helping to achieve the programming objectives of your organization.

2.4 In-House Advertising

Put up posters, create displays, and use your organization's Web site to promote programs inside your organization. You can also make flyers or brochures to outline the programs you offer. Figure 6.4 is a brochure of children's programs offered by a community library. These brochures should be distributed from every public service point in your institution—especially in the children's room. You can also mail out these flyers to community agencies that serve a clientele you want to reach. Doctor's offices, social service agencies, supermarkets, and neighbourhood associations will often carry a selection of your brochures for their clients to pick up. Many libraries regularly mail newsletters to patrons to let them know all the up-and-coming events. You can have patrons sign up to be on the mailing list and send them seasonal flyers on a regular basis. Many libraries also send virtual newsletters and announcements for upcoming events by compiling e-mail lists. Ask people if they would be interested in receiving information about upcoming programs on your institution's Web site. Compile a list of e-mail addresses and send an electronic copy of your program flyer. Be sure to design the flyer in a standard format that most computer users can view, such as the Web-ready html format or Adobe's .pdf format.

Use publicity to make your programs more effective and to reach as many people in your community as possible. Publicity takes some significant time to establish, but once you have the formula in place, you can use it over and over as you add programs and run special events.

2.5 Web Site Features

If your organization has a Web site, you can use it to feature news and information about upcoming events. Most libraries have Internet access to the library catalogue, and patrons will log in regularly to check for materials in the library. Take advantage of this access by featuring upcoming events prominently on the library's home page where people are likely to see it. Don't clutter the page with too much information; people will be overwhelmed and more likely to ignore everything. Instead, prominently feature a few key messages that you want to get across. Visit the Cambridge Libraries Web site (www.cambridge.libraries.ca) for examples.

3. Outreach

In the first section of this chapter, several questions were outlined to help you develop a marketing and promotion campaign. Two of these questions were

- Whom are you trying to reach?

- What obstacles stand in the way of these people attending your programs?

You will likely realize when answering these questions that some of the people you are trying to reach are unable to come to your facility because they are not mobile. Children in daycare and preschool throughout the day will not be able to attend programs designed for individual children. Some families, whose economic circumstances do not allow them to have a car, may be unable to reach your facility. How can you reach those people? You may choose to bring literacy out into the community for these organizations. If you decide to do outreach as a means of promotion for in-house library activities, however, it is *not* effective to speak to groups of children. It is more effective to speak to groups of adults, or adults with children. Contact local television talk shows and news organizations and offer to speak or do a promotional spot. Look for groups of parents gathered in one place—playgroups, sports activities, PTA meetings. These community venues will give you a chance to speak to groups of parents and promote the library's programs.

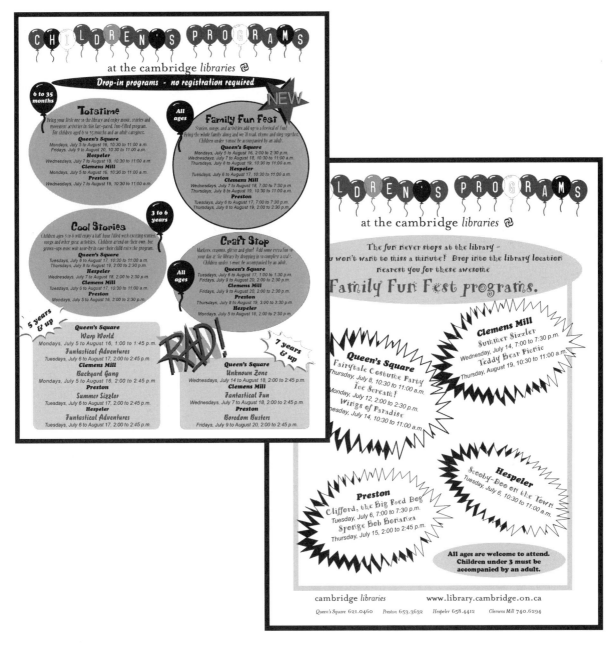

Figure 6-4. Library Children's Programming Flyer (Two-Page Spread)

Many facilities do outreach to preschools and elementary schools as a means of bringing the library into the community, and this is a valuable service. However, it is not a valuable promotional tool unless you have flyers and brochures for children to bring home. If you do a program at a local school, time it to precede your library's program registration and bring flyers along to promote your programs. Ask teachers to put the flyers in with other messages to go home and, hopefully, parents will take the time to review your flyer and see the programs your facility has to offer.

4. Community Partnerships

Establishing relationships with other groups in your community will allow you to expand your audience base to include these other groups' clientele. Take a look at businesses and facilities in your community and think creatively to come up with programs you can do together. Examples of organizations approached and creative community partnerships that have worked as a means of promotion follow.

- **Local Children's Clothing or Toy Store**—Offer to read stories at your local children's stores at a given time once per month. Children will gather and adults will be able to shop unencumbered for a little while. Pass out flyers and tell parents about preschool storytimes and other age-appropriate programs you have to offer.

- **Hardware Store**—With the local hardware store supplying the materials and space, promote a program for children to learn how to make a simple woodworking project, taken from a children's nonfiction book. Use the time to talk to parents and others in the store to promote library programs and services.

- **Neighbourhood Associations and Community Centres**—Working together, you can plan a family literacy night and bring in a crowd from the community. Discuss with parents the role they play in their child's path to literacy. Play word games and read to the children. Give out flyers and discuss how library programs meet literacy objectives.

- **Coffee Shops**—Have storytime at the local coffee shop once a month. Give out flyers to parents lucky enough to enjoy an uninterrupted cup of coffee while their children were entertained.

These are just a few examples of ways librarians have gone out into the community to focus attention on programs and resources they have to offer. Look at a business directory or information guide for your community and brainstorm on agencies that may enjoy mutually beneficial relationships with the library.

5. Gathering Statistics

Now that you have a program line-up you are happy with and you have spent some time and energy designing effective publicity, you need to make a case for the continued level of monetary and staffing support that is needed to maintain programs. Statistics are a valuable way to assess the need for new programs and to justify current programming. Statistics may also show that some programs are no longer needed, and you may see an opportunity to update your programming line-up. There are a number of useful ways to gather program statistics. If you are considering adding or dropping a program, or if you are asked to prepare a report on a program's effectiveness, you need to asses more than the number of children who attend a program each week. Although simple numerical program statistics are important and effective for demonstrating the success of an individual program, they do not help to assess the need for new programs or a shift in the focus or concentration of programming.

5.1 Population and Community Demographics

Learn about the people in your neighbourhood. How old are they? How many children do they have? What are the children's ages? What languages do the families speak? What is their educational background? These are just a few of the questions that can be answered with census information and can help to design your programming line-up or help make a case for additional programs. Government information on people in your community can be obtained from a number of different sources. In Canada, Statistics Canada is a government organization that publishes census information (Statistics Canada, 2004). In the United States, the U.S. Census Bureau publishes this information, including the *American Community Survey* (U.S. Census Bureau, 2004). Visit the Census Bureau or Statistics Canada Web sites to find more information about your community or area of the country. By learning about the people who make up your community's population you can make informed decisions about the programs you'd like to offer them.

5.2 Surveys

If you need specific information to help you gauge the need for a program, you can conduct a survey. There are a number of important things to think about when you are planning a survey. The following are a few factors you should consider:

- What, *exactly*, are you trying to find out about the members of your community?

- What questions can you ask that will elicit appropriate responses without leading participants to a preselected answer?

- Whom will you ask; what specific users are you interested in identifying?

- What is the best time to get a good selection of those users to fill out your survey?

- How many surveys will you need completed to achieve a reliable result?

- How will you tabulate the results of your survey?

- Is it useful to include qualitative results, opinions, and comments in your survey?

- How will you use the information once it is gathered?

These are just a few of the general considerations. If you are planning a survey, before you spend a great deal of money or staff time, you may want to invest in the professional help of a polling agency to assist with survey design.

5.3 Evaluations

Every program should include a medium for participants to evaluate the results of the program. Programs, special events, and workshops all should be followed with a feedback form for participants. Have the feedback form relate to the goals and objectives of the program (see figure 6.5 for a sample evaluation form). Consider using positive feedback and comments to "sell" your programs with a testimonial flyer. Gather comments and arrange them in an attractive way as you often see done in advertising for a movie or novel. Include the most positive and interesting comments. Send the testimonial flyers to groups or prospective participants whom you feel you are not reaching with the traditional forms of publicity.

Children's Services

Program Evaluation Form

At the Cambridge Libraries we continually strive to improve our children's programs. Your input on the program your child recently attended will assist us with this process.

Program Attended : ☐ The Story Corner   ☐ Afterschool Adventures   ☐ Family Storytime

Please circle the answer that best describes the experience your child had in this program:

What was your child's overall impression of this program?	*poor*	*fair*	*satisfactory*	*good*	*excellent*	*not applicable*
What is your child's impression of the stories shared in this program?	*poor*	*fair*	*satisfactory*	*good*	*excellent*	*not applicable*
What was your child's impression of the books displayed to take home?	*poor*	*fair*	*satisfactory*	*good*	*excellent*	*not applicable*
What was your child's impression of the other activities included in this program (games, crafts, etc.)?	*poor*	*fair*	*satisfactory*	*good*	*excellent*	*not applicable*
How would you rate the age-appropriateness of this program?	*poor*	*fair*	*satisfactory*	*good*	*excellent*	*not applicable*

Please circle yes or no for the following questions:

Did your child have a positive experience in this program?   yes   no
If no, why not? _____
_____

Did your child take books or other library materials home from this program?   yes   no
If no, why not? _____
_____

Would you register your child for another library program based on this experience?   yes   no
If no, why not? _____
_____

Do you feel the total number of children registered for this program was appropriate?   yes   no
If no, why not? _____
_____

Please add any additional comments:
_____
_____
_____
_____
_____
_____
_____

Figure 6.5. Program Evaluation Form

6. Continued Success

Through consistent evaluation and statistical scrutiny, you will see whether your programs are meeting the objectives you have set for them. With the right combination of planning, publicity, and personality you will likely enjoy continued success. To maintain a level of success, keep ideas fresh and staff rejuvenated. Go to workshops, presentations, and conferences if they are available in your area. Read how other libraries achieve programming success and learn from their encounters. Network and make contacts and share your ideas and information. Book-based programming can have a significant impact on the value of the library in your community, early literacy, and children's well-being, so continually work on making it the best it can be for everyone involved.

Suggested Reading

Emergent Literacy and Literacy

Baker, Betty, et al. 1998. Reading Awareness: An Evolving Success. *Illinois Libraries* 80:2 (Spring 1998): 84–86.

Berg, Leila. 1977. *Reading and Loving.* London: Routledge & Kegan Paul.

Carlson, Ann D. 1985. *Early Childhood Literature Sharing Programs in Libraries.* Hamden, CT: Library Professional Publications.

Carlson, Ann D. 1992. *The Preschooler and the Library.* Metuchen, NJ: Scarecrow Press.

Crago, Maureen, and Hugh Crago. 1983. *Prelude to Literacy: A Preschool Child's Encounter With Picture and Story.* Carbondale: Southern Illinois University Press.

Cullinan, Bernice E. 1992. *Read to Me: Raising Kids Who Love to Read.* New York: Scholastic.

Fox, Mem. 2001. *Reading Magic: Why Reading Aloud to Our Children Will Change Their Lives Forever.* San Diego: Harcourt Brace.

Glazer, Susan Mandel. 1980. *Getting Ready to Read: Creating Readers from Birth Through Six.* Englewood Cliffs, NJ: Prentice-Hall.

Kropp, Paul. 2000. *How to Make Your Child a Reader for Life.* New York: Broadway Books.

Kropp, Paul. 1996. *Raising a Reader: Make Your Child a Reader for Life.* New York: Doubleday.

Mustard, Fraser. 1999. *Reversing the Real Brain Drain: Early Years Study: Final Report.* Toronto: Canadian Institute for Advanced Research.

Preschool Services and Parent Education Committee, Association for Library Service to Children. 1990. *First Steps to Literacy: Library Programs for Parents, Teachers, and Caregivers.* Chicago: American Library Association.

Walter, Virginia A. 2001. *Children & Libraries: Getting It Right.* Chicago: American Library Association.

Sample Programs and Program Planning

Arnold, Renea. 2004. A Script for Success: Talking Points Can Make Storytime a Much Richer Experience for Everyone. *School Library Journal* (September).

Batluck, Naomi. 1993. *Crazy Gibberish: And Other Story Hour Stretches (From a Storyteller's Bag of Tricks).* Hamden, CT: Linnet Books.

Bauer, Caroline Feller. 1992. *Read for the Fun of It: Active Programming with Books for Children.* New York: The H. W. Wilson Company.

Beall, Pamela C. T. 1994. *Wee Sing Children's Songs and Fingerplays*. Los Angeles: Price Stern Sloan.

Briggs, Diane. 1997. *52 Programs for Preschoolers: The Librarian's Year-Round Planner*. Chicago: American Library Association.

Brouse, Ann. 1999. *Talk It Up! Book Discussion Programs for Young People*. Albany: New York Library Association.

Castellano, Marie. 2003. *Simply Super Storytimes*. Fort Atkinson, WI: Upstart Books.

Cobb, Jane. 1996. *I'm a Little Teapot!: Presenting Preschool Storytime*. Vancouver, BC: Black Sheep Press.

Dailey, Susan. 2001. A *Storytime Year: A Month-to-Month Kit for Preschool Programming*. New York: Neal-Schuman.

Friedes, Harriet. 1993. *The Preschool Resource Guide: Educating and Entertaining Children Aged Two Through Five*. New York: Plenum Press.

Kladder, Jeri. 1995. *Story Hour: 55 Preschool Programs for Public Libraries*. Jefferson, NC: McFarland.

Lerach, Helen. 1993. *Creative Storytimes*. Regina, SK: Regina Public Library.

MacDonald, Margaret Read. 1995. *Bookplay: 101 Creative Themes to Share with Young Children*. North Haven, CT: Library Professional Publications.

MacDonald, Margaret Read. 1988. *Booksharing: 101 Programs to Use with Preschoolers*. Hamden, CT: Library Professional Publications.

Maddigan, Beth, Stefanie Drennan, and Roberta Thompson. 2003. *The BIG Book of Stories, Songs, and Sing-Alongs: Programs for Babies, Toddlers, and Families*. Westport, CT: Libraries Unlimited.

Nespeca, Sue McCleaf. 1994. *Library Programming for Families with Young Children*. New York: Neal-Schuman.

Oakes, Susan. 2001. Animal Crackers, Milk, and a Good Book: Creating a Successful Early Childhood Literacy Program. *Public Libraries* 40:3 (May/June): 166–69.

1001 Rhymes & Fingerplays for Working with Young Children. 1994. Everett, WA: Warren Publishing House.

Reid, Rob. 1995. *Children's Jukebox: A Subject Guide to Musical Recordings and Programming Ideas for Songsters Ages One to Twelve*. Chicago: American Library Association.

Reid, Rob. 1999. *Family Storytime: Twenty-Four Creative Programs for All Ages*. Chicago: American Library Association.

Ring a Ring O' Roses: Stories, Games and Fingerplays for Preschool Children. Rev. ed. 1977. Flint, MI: Flint Public Library.

Sierra, Judy. 1997. *The Flannel Board Storytelling Book*. New York: H. W. Wilson.

Silberg, Jackie. 2002. *The Complete Book of Rhymes, Songs, Poems, Fingerplays, and Chants: Over 700 Selections*. Beltsville, MD: Gryphon House.

Sitarz, Paula Gaj. 1990. *More Picture Book Story Hours: From Parties to Pets.* Englewood, CO: Libraries Unlimited.

Warren, Jean. 1983. *Piggyback Songs: New Songs Sung to the Tunes of Childhood Favorites.* Everett, WA: Totline Press; Warren Publishing House.

Weissman, "Miss Jackie". 1991. *Higglety, Pigglety, Pop! 233 Playful Rhymes and Chants for Your Baby.* Overland Park, KS: Miss Jackie Music Co.

Woboditsch, Mary. 1995. *You Asked for It: A Guide to Storyhours.* Lively, ON: Walden Public Library.

Child Development

Allen, K. Eileen, and Lynn R. Marotz. 2000. *By the Ages: Behavior & Development of Children Pre-Birth Through Eight.* Albany, NY: Delmar Thomson Learning.

Bredekamp, Sue, ed. 1987. *Developmentally Appropriate Practice in Early Childhood Programs Serving Children from Birth Through Age 8.* Washington, DC: National Association for the Education of Young Children.

Schaefer, Charles E., and Theresa Foy DiGeronimo. 2000. *Ages and Stages: A Parent's Guide to Normal Childhood Development.* New York: John Wiley.

Thomas, R. Murray. 1992. *Comparing Theories of Child Development.* Belmont, CA: Wadsworth.

What a Child Will Be Depends on You and Me: A Resource Kit for a Child's First Five Years. 2001. Toronto: Invest in Kids Foundation.

Library Children's Services

Fasick, Adele. 1998. *Managing Children's Services in the Public Library.* Englewood, CO: Libraries Unlimited.

Feinberg, Sandra. 1998. *Learning Environments for Young Children: Rethinking Library Spaces and Services.* Chicago: American Library Association.

Gerhardt, Lillian, ed. 1997. *School Library Journal's Best: A Reader for Children's, Young Adult and School Librarians.* New York: Neal-Schuman.

Kids Welcome Here!: Writing Public Library Policies That Promote Use by Young People. 1990. Edited by Anne E. Simon. Albany: Youth Services Section, New York Library Association.

Phares, Carol. 2001. Super Duper Program Planning. *Mississippi Libraries* 65:3 (Fall): 74–77.

Reif, Kathleen. 2000. Are Public Libraries the Preschooler's Door to Learning? *Public Libraries* 39:5 (September/October): 262–68.

Rollock, Barbara T. 1988. *Public Library Services for Children.* Hamden, CT: Library Professional Publications.

Steele, Anita T. 2001. *Bare Bones Children's Services: Tips for Public Library Generalists.* Chicago: American Library Association.

Teale, William H. 1999. Libraries Promote Early Literacy Learning: Ideas from Current Research and Early Childhood Programs. *Journal of Youth Services in Libraries* 12:3 (Spring): 9–16.

Walter, Virginia A. 2001. *Children & Libraries: Getting It Right.* Chicago: American Library Association.

Children's Literature

Bettleheim, Bruno. 1977.*The Uses of Enchantment.* New York: Vintage Books.

Hilman, Judith. 1999. *Discovering Children's Literature.* 2d ed. New York: Prentice Hall.

Lynch-Brown, Carol, and Carl M. Tomlinson. 1999. *Essentials of Children's Literature.* 3d ed. Boston: Allyn and Bacon.

Sutherland, Zena. 1997. *Children & Books.* New York: Longman.

Bibliographies and Booklists

Association for Library Service to Children. 2001. *The New Books Kids Like.* Chicago: American Library Association.

Baker, Deidre, and Ken Setterington. 2003. *A Guide to Canadian Children's Books.* Totonto: McClelland & Stewart .

Cullinan, Bernice E. 1993. *Let's Read About . . . : Finding Books They'll Love to Read.* New York: Scholastic.

Cullum, Carolyn. 1999. *The Storytime Sourcebook: A Compendium of Ideas and Resources for Storytellers.* New York: Neal-Schuman.

Landsberg, Michele. 1986. *Michele Landsberg's Guide to Children's Books: With a Treasury of More Than 350 Great Children's Books.* Markham, ON: Penguin Books.

Lipson, Eden Ross. 2000. *The New York Times Parent's Guide to the Best Books for Children.* New York: Three Rivers Press.

McGovern, Edythe M., and Helen D. Muller. 1994. *They're Never Too Young for Books: A Guide to Children's Books for Ages 1 to 8.* Buffalo, NY: Prometheus Books.

Thomas, James L. 1992. *Play, Learn, and Grow: An Annotated Guide to the Best Books and Materials for Very Young Children.* New Providence, NJ: R. R. Bowker.

Other

Statistics Canada. 2004. *2001 Community Profiles.* Ottawa, ON: Statistics Canada. Available at www.statcan.ca/english.

U.S. Census Bureau, Demographic Surveys Division. 2004. *American Community Survey.* Washington, DC: U.S. Census Bureau. Available at http://www.census.gov/.

Author/Title Index

191

Subject Index

About the Authors

BETH MADDIGAN is Coordinator of Children's Services at Cambridge Libraries & Galleries, Cambridge, Ontario.

STEFANIE DRENNAN, a mom to three beautiful daughters, is an Early Childhood Education Teacher and currently the Supervisor of Greenbrook Co-Operative Preschool in Kitchener, Ontario.

ROBERTA THOMPSON, a former Camgridge Libraries staff member, is a freelance illustrator in British Columbia, Canada.

DEC   2009